# Cambridge Elements

Elements in Decision Theory and Philosophy
edited by
Martin Peterson
*Texas A&M University*

# SMALL PROBABILITIES AND HIGH STAKES

Christian Tarsney
*University of Toronto*

CAMBRIDGE
UNIVERSITY PRESS

# CAMBRIDGE
## UNIVERSITY PRESS

Shaftesbury Road, Cambridge CB2 8EA, United Kingdom

One Liberty Plaza, 20th Floor, New York, NY 10006, USA

477 Williamstown Road, Port Melbourne, VIC 3207, Australia

314–321, 3rd Floor, Plot 3, Splendor Forum, Jasola District Centre,
New Delhi – 110025, India

Cambridge University Press is part of Cambridge University Press & Assessment,
a department of the University of Cambridge.

We share the University's mission to contribute to society through the pursuit of
education, learning and research at the highest international levels of excellence.

www.cambridge.org
Information on this title: www.cambridge.org/9781009571609

DOI: 10.1017/9781009333047

© Christian Tarsney 2026



When citing this work, please include a reference to the DOI 10.1017/9781009333047

First published 2026

*A catalogue record for this publication is available from the British Library*

*A Cataloging-in-Publication data record for this Element is available from the Library
of Congress*

ISBN 978-1-009-57160-9 Hardback
ISBN 978-1-009-33303-0 Paperback
ISSN 2517-4827 (online)
ISSN 2517-4819 (print)



For EU product safety concerns, contact us at Calle de José Abascal, 56, 1°, 28003
Madrid, Spain, or email eugpsr@cambridge.org

# Small Probabilities and High Stakes

Elements in Decision Theory and Philosophy

DOI: 10.1017/9781009333047
First published online: May 2026

Christian Tarsney
*University of Toronto*

**Author for correspondence:** Christian Tarsney, christian.tarsney@gmail.com

**Abstract:** What price should you be willing to pay for a tiny probability of an astronomically large gain, or to avoid a tiny probability of an astronomically large loss? Should you be willing to pay *any* finite price, if the potential gains or losses are large enough? *Fanaticism* says you should, while *anti-fanaticism* says you should not. Focusing on morally motivated decision-making, this Element explores arguments for and against both positions, ultimately defending the intermediate view that rationality permits a range of dispositions toward extreme risks, while ruling out the most comprehensive forms of both fanaticism and anti-fanaticism. The final section considers practical implications, arguing that under real-world circumstances, any view satisfying a minimal principle of rationality must very often rank options by expected value, and thus sometimes give great weight to intuitively small probabilities, but that we nonetheless retain rational flexibility in sufficiently extreme cases.

**Keywords:** fanaticism, extreme risk, low-probability risk, existential risk, population ethics



ISBNs: 9781009571609 (HB), 9781009333030 (PB), 9781009333047 (OC)
ISSNs: 2517-4827 (online), 2517-4819 (print)

# Contents

# 1 Introduction

Every 150 million years or so, the Earth is struck by a "planet killer" asteroid more than 10 kilometers wide. These impacts unleash almost unimaginable devastation, not just from the heat, shock waves, and seismic activity generated by the impact itself but by vaporizing vast quantities of rock that linger in the upper atmosphere, shrouding the planet in darkness and blocking photosynthesis for years on end. Famously, an impact of this kind 66 million years ago, just off the coast of the present-day Yucatán Peninsula, wiped out three quarters of all plant and animal species on Earth, including the non-avian dinosaurs.

Another such asteroid might, at this moment, be on course to strike our planet in the next century. This is very unlikely.[1] But if such an impact were allowed to occur, the consequences would be catastrophic, and could well include human extinction or the permanent end of human civilization. How much, then, should we be willing to spend to prepare for this remote possibility – for instance, to develop the infrastructure necessary to deflect a planet-killing asteroid, if needed?

Other extreme risks present us with questions of a similar flavor, though each with its own distinctive complications. Consider climate change, for instance. Climate change over the next couple of centuries is likely to be serious but survivable. But there's a small chance that feedback effects, for instance from melting permafrost or methane clathrate, lead to extreme warming of 6°C or more, which could pose a catastrophic threat to humanity (Wagner and Weitzman, 2015). How much *more* should we be willing to spend on mitigating climate change, because of this small risk of extreme warming, compared with what would be warranted if we just considered the most likely scenario?

Or consider the risk of global nuclear war. Unlike risks from planet-killer asteroids and extreme warming, this risk may be quite substantial over the next century. But for a typical person, doing anything about it is very difficult. Consider an altruistically motivated young person considering whether to pursue a career in her country's diplomatic service, with the aim of reducing risks from nuclear conflict. The chance that her pursuing that career would make the difference between a global nuclear war occurring or not is very small, so choosing to do so would only reduce the overall risk by a tiny amount; but the stakes, of course, are enormous. How much should this young person be willing to give

---

[1] Because we have managed to identify and track a large majority of the largest asteroids that might cross our orbit, this probability is significantly lower than the baseline probability of 1 in 1.5 million per century – perhaps 1 in 150 million or less (Ord, 2020, 71).

up, in terms of what she might accomplish in other careers, for the sake of that small change in probabilities?

In each of these cases, the costs required to slightly alter the probability of an extreme outcome are themselves morally serious. The money spent on developing asteroid defenses could instead be spent to save or improve lives. Aggressive climate change mitigation can slow economic development, prolonging poverty and likewise costing lives. And an altruistically motivated young person could spend her career in many ways that have a very substantial probability of doing significant good in the world.

All these cases are examples of what I'll call *extreme tradeoffs*. They involve tradeoffs between the *probability* of a good or bad thing on the one hand, and its *magnitude* on the other. For instance, preventing human extinction by spending a given sum of money on asteroid defense would be a much greater good than saving, say, 100 lives by spending the money on health services; but the probability of that good being realized is much smaller. Extreme tradeoffs involve a choice between two options, which we can call a *safe bet* and a *long shot*. In simple cases (and focusing on the case of goods rather than bads), the safe bet delivers some good outcome with certainty, while the long shot delivers an *extremely* good outcome with very small probability, and a bad or neutral outcome otherwise. More generally, as I will eventually have reason to emphasize, extreme tradeoffs involve choices between a sure *improvement* to the world and a small *shift* in probability from a much worse outcome to a much better outcome.[2]

The central question of this work is *how to evaluate extreme tradeoffs* – how much weight we should be willing to give to very small probabilities, or differences in probability, if the stakes are high enough.

A standard answer to this question, which will play a central role in our investigation, tells us to *maximize expected value*. The expected value of an option is found by taking the values of each of its possible outcomes (assumed to be representable by real numbers), multiplying the value of each outcome by its probability, and summing up the resulting terms. Expected value maximization tells us to rank our options based on these probability-weighted sums ("expectations"), choosing an option whose expectation is maximal.

Expected value maximization seems prone, in practice, to giving very great weight to small probabilities and differences in probability. Consider risks of human extinction, from sources like asteroids, climate change, or nuclear war. Avoiding human extinction in the next century would plausibly be *very good*.

---

[2]   For that reason, the title of this work is a slight oversimplification: It would be more accurate, though clunkier, to say that our topic is "small probability *differences* and high stakes."

How good? Well, consider what humanity might accomplish if we avoid extinction. Human life might continue on Earth for eons to come, allowing perhaps $10^{17}$ future human lives to be lived (10 billion lives per century, for the next billion years). These lives might be as good as or better than the best lives today, full of love, beauty, knowledge, fun, and anything else that makes life worth living. We might also someday spread to the stars, allowing a vastly greater number of such lives to be lived – perhaps $10^{30}$, perhaps far more (Bostrom, 2003, 2013).[3]

If we would in fact achieve such a future by avoiding extinction, and if potential future lives count for as much as existing lives, then the value of avoiding near-term human extinction is so vast that even intuitively tiny differences in the risk of extinction carry enormous expected value. Thus, for instance, Nick Bostrom concludes that even on (what he takes to be) a conservative estimate of the stakes, "the expected value of reducing existential risk by a mere *one millionth of one percentage point* is at least a hundred times the value of a million human lives" (Bostrom, 2013, 18–19). On this way of thinking, we should be willing to pay *enormous* costs to reduce extinction risks – for instance, foregoing opportunities to save or improve vast numbers of present lives for the sake of tiny reductions in risk. Despite the theoretical naturalness of expected value maximization, most people will find this sort of reasoning extremely counterintuitive. As we will see in the next section, if there are no upper and lower limits on the value of outcomes, then expected value maximization can be pushed to even more counterintuitive extremes in the context of extreme tradeoffs.

Small probabilities of extreme outcomes have played an important role in the history of decision theory, figuring in some of its earliest and most enduring puzzles, like Pascal's wager (Pascal, 1669) and the St. Petersburg paradox (Bernoulli, 1738). And the counterintuitiveness of giving potentially unlimited weight to arbitrarily low-probability outcomes has been a recurring observation, particularly in the context of a running debate within expected utility theory about whether rational utility functions must be bounded (e.g., Aumann, 1977, 444; Machina, 1982, 283–284).

But recently the question of whether we should give potentially unlimited weight to arbitrarily small probabilities has begun to receive more focused attention from philosophers, as a topic that generalizes beyond particular puzzle cases and beyond the context of expected utility theory. This recent literature

---

[3] Human extinction will be a central example of an extreme, high-stakes outcome throughout this work. I will take for granted that human extinction would be bad, although of course that's open to dispute. The question of whether human extinction would be *astronomically* bad, as the numbers in the main text suggest, will be discussed in Section 8.2.

has centered on a thesis that has come to be called *fanaticism*. Fanaticism asserts, very roughly, that arbitrarily small probabilities can carry arbitrarily great weight in evaluation or decision-making, if the stakes are high enough.[4] This interest in fanaticism has been largely motivated by the growing significance of small-probability, high-stakes considerations in practical ethics (especially in debates over the moral importance of catastrophic risks). The recent literature includes defenses of fanaticism and closely related theses (Wilkinson, 2022, 2024; Goodsell, 2024; Kowalczyk, forthcoming), expressions of skepticism and attempts to avoid fanaticism (Balfour, 2021; Temkin, 2022, Appendix A; Bottomley and Williamson, 2025; Hong, 2025), as well as careful nonpartisan analyses of the arguments on either side (Russell, 2023; Beckstead and Thomas, 2024). The debate over fanaticism has also been paralleled by a renewed interest in the opposing idea of "small-probability discounting," that sufficiently small probabilities either can or should be simply ignored for purposes of decision-making, which has been recently defended by Smith (2014) and Monton (2019), and criticized by Isaacs (2016), Cibinel (2023), and Kosonen (2024), among others.

We will approach the general question of how to evaluate extreme tradeoffs primarily by asking whether we should accept or reject fanaticism and various alternative theses. As in most of the recent literature on fanaticism, our primary focus will be on *morally motivated* decisions (including the decisions of a policymaker or "social planner" motivated by social welfare). First, this is where the central question arises most forcefully. Choices that affect many individuals are potentially much higher-stakes than choices that affect only one; and on the other hand, given the scale and complexity of the social world, affecting those high-stakes outcomes can be very difficult, and so particularly prone to generating very small effects on the probability of some outcome of interest (like human extinction). Second, as we'll see in Section 3, the strongest argument for fanaticism essentially concerns actions that affect a potentially very large number of individuals. That said, many of the arguments we consider will also be applicable to individual prudential decision-making.

A final caveat: There are many interesting topics and literatures related to extreme tradeoffs that I won't have space to explore. Perhaps the most significant is the possibility of outcomes that are *infinitely* desirable or undesirable, like eternal salvation in Pascal's Wager, in the sense that any change

---

[4] This use of "fanaticism" seems to derive from slightly different uses in Ross (2006) (who's focused on small probabilities assigned to unreasonably extreme moral theories, in the context of decision-making under moral uncertainty) and Bostrom (2011) (who uses it to describe the idea that any non-zero probability of *infinite* goods or bads outweighs any finite good or bad, a thesis that Beckstead and Thomas (2024) have more recently dubbed "infinity obsession").

in their probabilities should take precedence over all ordinary considerations. Some other notable omissions include the distinctive issues arising from absolutist nonconsequentialism (involving tiny risks of violating absolute moral constraints) and from moral uncertainty (involving tiny credences in unreasonably extreme moral theories), extensions of expected value theory to evaluate prospects without finite expectations, like the St. Petersburg game, and debates over the "precautionary principle." Lastly, while we'll discuss one practical context where extreme tradeoffs arise (in Section 8), there are many others we won't have space to discuss that raise independently interesting issues: for instance, the impact of individual contributions in contexts like voting, factory farming, and climate change; tail risks in finance; and the details of specific catastrophic risks like asteroids, climate change, and nuclear war.

So, here's the plan: Section 2 will give formal statements of fanaticism and of the contrary thesis of *anti-fanaticism*, and explain the relationship between fanaticism and the principles of *expected value maximization* and *expected utility maximization*. Section 3 then sets out two arguments for fanaticism. While these arguments are both potentially compelling, I'll explain why I'm ultimately unconvinced by them. In Section 4, we'll see that there's also a compelling argument *against* fanaticism, based on its capacity to generate paradoxical gambles akin to the St. Petersburg game. Section 5 shows how this argument can be extended to a positive argument for a version of anti-fanaticism. But Section 6 shows that there's a compelling argument against anti-fanaticism as well: Trying to avoid fanaticism in full generality leads all-but-inevitably to an incoherent, cyclic ranking of prospects. To synthesize these conflicting arguments, Section 7 outlines and defends an intermediate, "permissivist" position, which is my central positive thesis. According to this view, rationality permits a range of attitudes toward extreme tradeoffs, from fairly fanatical to fairly anti-fanatical, while ruling out the most comprehensive forms of both fanaticism and anti-fanaticism.

Finally, in Section 8, I'll turn from theory to practice, exploring the real-world significance of small probabilities and high stakes in a practical context that has figured centrally in recent debates, the context of *altruistic prioritization*. I'll argue that, in this context, small effects on the probabilities of extreme outcomes may well be the primary determinants of expected value, so that expected value maximizers at least should often go for long shots over safe bets. I'll also argue that, given our "background uncertainty" about morally significant features of the world unaffected by our choices, even permissive and anti-fanatical decision theories will often – though not always – agree with expected value maximization in practice. The result is a picture intermediate between fanaticism and anti-fanaticism, vindicating many instances of expected value reasoning even in extreme tradeoffs, while avoiding its most counterintuitive extremes. I'll close in Section 9 by briefly summing up this mixed picture.

## 2 Fanaticism and Anti-Fanaticism

Before we get to the good stuff, we need to do some stage-setting. So, Section 2.1 will lay out a basic conceptual and formal framework. Sections 2.2 – 2.4 will use that framework to give initial formal statements of fanaticism, anti-fanaticism, and permissivism. Finally, Section 2.5 will formally introduce and contrast two ideas that will play a central role in the subsequent discussion: *expected value* and *expected utility*.

### 2.1 Setup: Outcomes, Prospects, and Preferences

Our central question is how agents should rank and choose between uncertain alternatives, in the context of extreme tradeoffs. I will call these alternatives *prospects*, and understand them as probability distributions over *outcomes*.[5]

An *outcome* is a specification of all evaluatively significant features of a possible world. For now, and in some of the following arguments, we will rely only on this characterization of outcomes. But in Section 3.2, I'll give outcomes some structure, representing them as assignments of "local" outcomes to a set of possible "value locations." The domain of possible outcomes is denoted $\mathbb{O}$.

We will restrict our attention to *finite* outcomes – thus, every instance of "outcome" can be read as shorthand for "finite outcome." This restriction is common in the literature on fanaticism; one motivation is to ensure that, for instance, an agent who regards some infinite outcomes (e.g., eternity in Heaven/Hell) as maximally good/bad can still count as fanatical. I won't try to draw a precise line between "finite" and "infinite" outcomes, but roughly, a finite outcome is one in which all evaluatively significant extensive quantities, like the number of welfare subjects and the durations of their lives, are finite.

Next, I assume that outcomes can be compared in terms of value. Formally, I'll assume a total preorder (a reflexive, transitive, and complete binary relation) $\succsim_{\mathbb{O}}$ on $\mathbb{O}$, where $o_i \succsim_{\mathbb{O}} o_j$ means that $o_i$ is *at least as good as* $o_j$.[6] If $o_i \succsim_{\mathbb{O}} o_j$

---

[5] It's common in decision theory to describe a situation where an agent can assign precise probabilities to decision-relevant possibilities as one of "risk," reserving "uncertainty" for situations where precise probabilities are unavailable. But since we'll be working entirely in the former context, I will disregard this distinction and use "uncertainty" in its ordinary English sense to indicate merely the absence of certainty.

[6] The assumption that the evaluative ordering of outcomes is complete is a convenient simplification rather than a substantive commitment. Our central question concerns gambles over rankable sets of outcomes: Should we prefer a *slightly* better outcome with certainty, or a small

but $o_j \not\succsim_O o_i$, then $o_i$ is *strictly better* than $o_j$, denoted $o_i \succ_O o_j$. If $o_i \succsim_O o_j$ and $o_j \succsim_O o_i$, then $o_i$ and $o_j$ are *equally good*, denoted $o_i \sim_O o_j$. In general, I'll understand these as relations of *impersonal* or *moral* value, but many of the arguments discussed in later sections are compatible with other interpretations (e.g., prudential).

A *prospect* is a probability distribution over outcomes. More specifically, we'll focus on *discrete* prospects, which assign non-zero probabilities to a finite or countably infinite set of outcomes, with those probabilities summing to 1. Such a prospect can be written as a sequence of ordered pairs $\langle (o_1, p_1), (o_2, p_2), \ldots \rangle$, where $(o_i, p_i)$ indicates that outcome $o_i$ occurs with probability $p_i$. Many of the arguments below will concern *binary* prospects, with two possible outcomes. Here I use the abbreviated notation $\langle o_i, p, o_j \rangle$ for the prospect that yields $o_i$ with probability $p$ and $o_j$ otherwise. A prospect that yields a single outcome $o_i$ with certainty is denoted $\langle o_i \rangle$. The domain of prospects we're interested in evaluating is denoted $\mathbb{P}$. I'll take for granted, as a background assumption in all the formal arguments below, that this domain includes at least all *finitely supported* prospects, that is, prospects that assign non-zero probability to only finitely many outcomes. At some points, I'll explicitly assume that the domain of prospects also includes some prospects with infinitely many possible outcomes.

In giving examples, I'll sometimes make informal reference to *states of nature* (or simply *states*). A state of nature specifies the features of the external environment that determine the outcome of an agent's choice (e.g., what asteroids, if any, are presently on a collision course for Earth). Given a set of mutually exclusive and jointly exhaustive states of nature, with probabilities assigned to them, prospects can be represented as functions from states to outcomes, specifying which outcome occurs in which state. While this way of representing prospects is sometimes explanatorily useful, the notion of states won't play any essential role in the formal arguments we examine.[7]

In understanding prospects as simple probability distributions over outcomes, I'm making two significant assumptions. First, I'm assuming that an agent can and should assign precise probabilities to particular outcomes, on

---

increase in the probability of a *vastly* better outcome? And it's simpler to assume that outcomes in general are completely ordered than to continually restate that the particular three or four outcomes under consideration are completely ordered.

[7] In particular, those arguments won't make use of the central piece of information that is added by representing prospects as functions from states to outcomes rather than simple probability measures – namely, whether two possible outcomes of two different prospects occur in the same state or different states. We'll occasionally make reference to *statewise dominance* principles, which do attach significance to this information, but those principles won't figure in the central arguments we examine.

the supposition that she chooses one or another risky alternative (even if those probabilities are highly subjective). Second, I'm assuming that the desirability of a prospect doesn't (or shouldn't) depend on which state of nature any given outcome occurs in. This assumption is disputable, but is licensed by the principle of Stochastic Dominance introduced and defended in Section 4.[8]

The final piece of our conceptual framework is the agent's *preference ranking* of prospects. Formally, an agent's preferences are represented by a relation $\succsim$ (assumed to be reflexive, but not necessarily transitive), where $P_i \succsim P_j$ means that prospect $P_i$ is *preferred at least equally* (or *weakly preferred*) to prospect $P_j$. If $P_i \succsim P_j$ but $P_j \not\succsim P_i$, then $P_i$ is *strictly preferred* to $P_j$, denoted $P_i > P_j$. If $P_i \succsim P_j$ and $P_j \succsim P_i$, then the two prospects are *equally preferred*, denoted $P_i \sim P_j$. If neither relation holds, then there is a *preference gap* between $P_i$ and $P_j$, denoted $P_i \bowtie P_j$.[9]

Our central interest will be in the *requirements of rationality* with respect to an agent's preferences between prospects.[10] More specifically, our focus will be on *ideal* rationality, the rational requirements that apply to an agent without cognitive limitations, and that (I take it) bounded agents like ourselves should in some sense aim to approximate. And we will focus on the rational requirements that apply to an agent who knows all the moral and other normative facts relevant to her situation, setting aside the question of how rational requirements might depend on our normative beliefs and uncertainties. Fanaticism and anti-fanaticism, as I will understand them, are conflicting theses about these idealized rational requirements. Our conceptual framework in hand, we can now give our first precise formulations of both theses.

---

[8] Moreover, the main (though not the only) point of controversy regarding this assumption concerns prospects with incomparable outcomes, and is sidestepped by restricting ourselves to a context in which all possible outcomes of the prospects under consideration can be compared.

[9] For now, I won't take any stance on what exactly "preferences" are (e.g., choice dispositions, subjective value judgments, beliefs about objective value...). I will only assume, informally, that preferences have some sort of connection to choice at least in agents who satisfy the requirements of rationality, so that the question of what preference one rationally ought to have between two prospects is closely tied to the question of which prospect one rationally ought to choose in a binary choice. In Section 7, I'll sketch my own preferred understanding of preferences, on which they amount to a sort of intention.

[10] Philosophers sometimes debate whether morally important choices under uncertainty should be assessed according to *moral* standards, *rational* standards, or both. I confess that I don't really understand this controversy, except insofar as it reflects the mistaken idea that rationality is distinctively associated with prudence, self-interest, or the satisfaction of an agent's subjective preferences. (I agree with J. J. C. Smart in "conceiv[ing] of ethics as the study of how it would be most rational to act" (Smart, 1956, 353).) So, while I will frame things in terms of rationality, I would be happy for the reader to substitute a concept like *subjective moral rightness* for *rationality* throughout, or to assume we're asking what would be rational for a *morally motivated* agent (excepting the occasional passages that consider fanaticism, anti-fanaticism, etc as theses about prudential rationality).

## 2.2 Fanaticism

Throughout this work, I'll use *fanaticism* (lowercase) to denote the informal idea that one should be willing to give arbitrarily large weight to arbitrarily small probabilities or differences in probability, if the stakes are high enough. And I will use *anti-fanaticism* (lowercase) to denote the informal idea that one should be willing to give only limited weight to probabilities or differences in probability below a certain size, no matter the stakes. We will introduce multiple precisifications of both theses, to which we will give capitalized names.

Let's begin, then, with a formal statement of a version of fanaticism. Like other forms of fanaticism and anti-fanaticism we will encounter, this formal thesis has both a "positive" component (concerning, roughly, choices between certainty of a fixed gain and a small probability of an indefinitely large gain) and a "negative" component (concerning, roughly, choices between certainty of a fixed loss and a small probability of an indefinitely large loss).

**Narrow Positive Fanaticism** It is rationally required that, for any outcomes $o^+ \succ_0 o^-$ and probability $p > 0$, there is an outcome $o^{*+}$ such that $\langle o^{*+}, p', o^- \rangle > \langle o^+ \rangle$ for all $p' \geq p$.

**Narrow Negative Fanaticism** It is rationally required that, for any outcomes $o^+ \succ_0 o^-$ and probability $p > 0$, there is an outcome $o^{*-}$ such that $\langle o^- \rangle > \langle o^{*-}, p', o^+ \rangle$ for all $p' \geq p$.[11]

Narrow Fanaticism is the conjunction of Narrow Positive Fanaticism and Narrow Negative Fanaticism. I call it "narrow" because it concerns a restricted category of extreme tradeoffs where one prospect delivers a single outcome with certainty; in Section 6 we'll consider a more general context where both prospects involve uncertainty.

An agent who satisfies Narrow Positive Fanaticism will forego certainty of a very good outcome, $o^+$, for a risky prospect that is almost certain to yield a very bad outcome $o^-$ but carries some minuscule probability of an outcome $o^{*+}$ – as long as $o^{*+}$ is good enough. An agent who satisfies Narrow Negative Fanaticism will *accept* certainty of the very bad outcome $o^-$, rather than take a risky prospect that is almost certain to deliver the very good outcome $o^+$, but carries some minuscule probability of an outcome $o^{*-}$ – as long as $o^{*-}$ is bad enough. Narrow Fanaticism does not say that any *particular* astronomically good/bad

---

[11] Here and elsewhere, I will use $o^+$ and $o^-$ to suggest good/bad outcomes, and $o^{*+}$ and $o^{*-}$ to suggest *astronomically* good/bad outcomes. These superscripts don't carry any formal meaning – they don't restrict quantification, for instance – but merely indicate what sort of outcome is of most interest, e.g., the cases in which a principle is interesting and nontrivial. Thus, for instance, a statement like "for any outcomes $o^+$ and $o^-$" can be read as "for any outcomes $o^+$ [no matter how good] and $o^-$ [no matter how bad]."

outcomes must count as "good enough"/"bad enough" in a given situation – it merely asserts that there must be *some* such outcomes.

As with other versions of fanaticism and anti-fanaticism we will consider, the positive and negative components of Narrow Fanaticism can come apart, and there is at least some intuitive motivation for accepting one without the other. (In particular, many will find the negative component of fanaticism less counterintuitive than the positive component.) But the formal arguments we consider in later sections will, in every case, apply identically to corresponding positive and negative theses.

Fanaticism strikes most people as deeply counterintuitive. To illustrate the point as starkly as possible, suppose that we face a collective choice between guaranteeing a very good future for all sentient life on Earth (say, hundreds of millions of years in which large populations will enjoy prosperity, justice, and happiness), or a gamble that gives us a one-in-a-googol ($10^{-100}$) chance of an *even better* collective future and a complementary ($1-10^{-100}$) probability of the instant and permanent annihilation of all life on Earth. Fanaticism implies that for *some* specification of the super-utopian future we would obtain by winning the gamble, we are required to choose it over certainty of mere utopia. Most of us will find this verdict very hard to accept.[12]

## 2.3 Anti-Fanaticism

Narrow Fanaticism holds that we are rationally required to give potentially unlimited weight to arbitrarily small probabilities of sufficiently extreme outcomes. A contrary thesis, Narrow Anti-Fanaticism, asserts the opposite requirement: We are rationally required to give only limited weight to sufficiently low-probability outcomes, no matter how high the stakes. It likewise consists of two theses:

**Narrow Positive Anti-Fanaticism**  It is rationally required that there are some outcomes $o^+ >_O o^-$ and probability $p > 0$ such that, for any outcome $o^{*+}$, $\langle o^+ \rangle > \langle o^{*+}, p', o^- \rangle$ for all $p' \leq p$.

**Narrow Negative Anti-Fanaticism**  It is rationally required that there are some outcomes $o^+ >_O o^-$ and probability $p > 0$ such that, for any outcome $o^{*-}$, $\langle o^{*-}, p', o^+ \rangle > \langle o^- \rangle$ for all $p' \leq p$.

---

[12] This example is taken from Tarsney (2025b). Similar illustrations of the counterintuitiveness of fanaticism (typically directed more specifically against unbounded expected value or expected utility maximization) include "Hurka's gamble" (Hurka, 1983), "Pascal's mugging" (Bostrom, 2009), and "Dyson's wager" (Wilkinson, 2022). The counterintuitiveness of expected value-driven fanaticism is also emphasized by Balfour (2021) and Temkin (2022, 351–352), among others.

An agent who satisfies Narrow Positive Anti-Fanaticism will at least sometimes prefer certainty of a very good outcome $o^+$ to a tiny chance of an astronomically good outcome $o^{*+}$ (and a very bad outcome $o^-$ otherwise), *no matter how good* $o^{*+}$ may be. On the other hand, an agent who satisfies Narrow Negative Anti-Fanaticism will sometimes prefer to take a tiny risk of an astronomically bad outcome $o^{*-}$ rather than settle for $o^-$, *no matter how bad $o^{*-}$* may be.

## 2.4 Permissivism

Fanaticism and anti-fanaticism (in the preceding formulations, and others that we will encounter later) assert contrary rational requirements. These rival theses are not jointly exhaustive, since rationality might impose *neither* requirement on us. I will use *permissivism* to denote any view which denies both that we are rationally required to have fanatical preferences and that we are rationally required to have anti-fanatical preferences. Permissivism can take multiple forms. For instance, it might permit both fanatical and anti-fanatical preferences. Or it might permit (or even, its name notwithstanding, require) *incomplete* preferences that are neither fanatical nor anti-fanatical. But apart from noting its existence, we will say no more about this third possibility for now, returning to it only in Section 7.

## 2.5 Expected Value and Expected Utility

Fanaticism is a thesis worth taking seriously, despite its counterintuitive implications, because there are substantial arguments in its favor. The most compelling arguments for fanaticism, which we will spell out formally in the next section, start from the idea that there are objective quantitative facts about the value of outcomes that constrain how agents should rank prospects. For instance, here's a simple argument for a certain kind of prudential fanaticism: "Suppose you are facing gambles where the prizes are extensions to your lifespan – more specifically, additional years of happy life, at some fixed level of happiness. The prudential value of a year of life just depends on how happy you are, not on how many years you have lived already. So two years of life at a fixed happiness level is twice as good as one year, three years is three times as good, and so on. Similarly, for any probability $p$, a $p$ chance of $n$ years of happy life is $n$ times as good as a $p$ chance of one year of happy life – meaning that you should be willing to pay $n$ times as much for such a chance. And surely, no matter how small $p$ is, you should be willing to pay *some* finite price (say, a fraction of a penny) for a $p$ chance of one additional happy life-year. But these claims together imply that, for any $p$ and any finite price, we can find some outcome (namely, a very large number of years of happy life) such that you are willing to pay that price for a $p$ chance of that outcome."

This argument illustrates the more general idea of *expected value maximization* (hereafter abbreviated MEV). MEV starts from the assumption that outcomes have cardinal degrees of value, independent of any agent's ranking of prospects, which can be represented by a *value function V* mapping each outcome to a real number.[13] The *expected value* of a prospect $P_j$ is the probability-weighted sum of the values of all its possible outcomes:

$$\mathbb{E}_V(P_j) = \sum_i P_j(o_i)V(o_i)$$

where $P_j(o_i)$ is the probability that $P_j$ yields outcome $o_i$.

MEV requires agents to rank prospects by expected value. More precisely, I will understand it to consist of the following claims:

**Maximize Expected Value (MEV)** It is rationally required that (i) if $\mathbb{E}_V(P_j) > \mathbb{E}_V(P_k)$, then $P_j \succ P_k$; and (ii) if $\mathbb{E}_V(P_j)$ and $\mathbb{E}_V(P_k)$ are both finite and $\mathbb{E}_V(P_j) = \mathbb{E}_V(P_k)$, then $P_j \sim P_k$.[14]

The informal argument for prudential fanaticism above claims that, all else being equal, the objective prudential value of an outcome increases linearly with the number of happy life-years the agent enjoys in that outcome, and that one should maximize expected value. If there is no upper limit to the number of happy life-years that it's possible for an individual to enjoy, then a prudential value function that increases linearly with happy life-years will be unbounded above, and maximizing the expectation of that value function entails Narrow Positive Fanaticism.

It's important to distinguish MEV from the weaker and more widely accepted idea of *expected utility maximization*.

---

[13] A bit more precisely, MEV requires that we can talk meaningfully about *ratios of value differences*, saying things like "the difference in value between $o_1$ and $o_2$ is $r$ times as large as the difference in value between $o_3$ and $o_4$" (and that this ratio $r$ is well-defined and finite for any quadruple of outcomes). This implies that the values of outcomes can be represented by real numbers in a way that's unique up to positive affine transformation, which is enough to guarantee that the ranking of outcomes in terms of expected value will not depend on our particular choice of numbers.

[14] I will assume that sums can take infinite values, when they diverge unconditionally to $+/-\infty$; thus, prospects can have infinite expected value (a point that we'll return to below, especially in Section 4). However, it's not plausible that we must be indifferent between any two prospects with infinite expectations of the same sign; hence, the indifference clause in MEV is restricted to finite expectations.

**Maximize Expected Utility (MEU)** It is rationally required that there is some function $U$ from outcomes to real numbers (a "utility function") such that (i) if $\mathbb{E}_U(P_j) > \mathbb{E}_U(P_k)$, then $P_j \succ P_k$; and (ii) if $\mathbb{E}_U(P_j)$ and $\mathbb{E}_U(P_k)$ are both finite and $\mathbb{E}_U(P_j) = \mathbb{E}_U(P_k)$, then $P_j \sim P_k$.

The requirement that an agent should rank prospects according to the expectation of *some* utility function is the central tenet of orthodox decision theory. It is typically defended on the grounds that an agent's preferences ought to satisfy a set of coherence constraints (e.g., the axioms of von Neumann and Morgenstern (1947) or Savage (1972)) which guarantee that the agent can be *represented as* maximizing the expectation of a utility function.

Even if there are cardinal facts about the values of outcomes, MEU in itself takes no cognizance of those facts. It just requires an agent to rank prospects according to the expectation of *some* utility function, which need not be identical with the objective value function or bear any particular relationship to it. In a moral context, though, it's natural to suppose that one rationally ought to prefer certainty of a better outcome to certainty of a worse outcome. (This principle will be stated officially in Section 6 under the name *Minimal Dominance*.) Combined with MEU, this means that one's utility function must be *increasing* with respect to the value of outcomes, assigning greater utility to better outcomes. And we will generally focus on utility functions that have this property.

Even within the constraint of assigning greater utility to better outcomes, however, MEU is much more permissive than MEV. To illustrate, consider a moral decision-making context in which lives are at risk, all of which have equal value, and the only morally relevant consideration is how many lives are saved or lost. In this context, it's natural to think that the value of an outcome (relative to a baseline in which no one is saved) is proportionate to the number of lives saved: saving two lives is twice as good as saving one, etc. If that's right, then MEV ranks prospects in this context by the expected number of lives saved, for example, preferring a prospect that saves 9 lives with probability 0.5 to a prospect that saves 4 lives with certainty. MEU does not give such precise verdicts. It allows an agent, for instance, to maximize the expected *square root* of lives saved, in which case she would prefer to save 4 lives for sure (with an expected utility of $1 \times \sqrt{4} = 2$) rather than 9 lives with probability 0.5 (with an expected utility of $0.5 \times \sqrt{9} + 0.5 \times 0 = 1.5$). In other words, MEV requires risk-neutrality with respect to lives saved, while MEU is compatible with risk aversion or risk seeking.

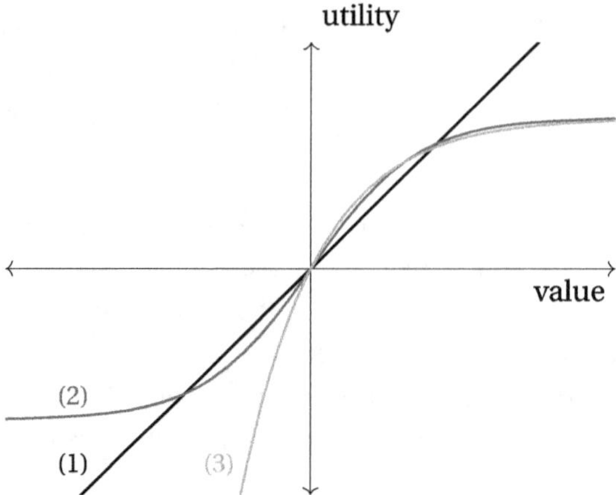



**Figure 1** Some increasing functions from value to utility: a linear function (1) that's unbounded above and below, an s-shaped function (2) that's bounded above and below, and an everywhere-concave function (3) that's bounded above but unbounded below.

Because MEV requires risk-neutrality with respect to a privileged value function, while MEU does not, these principles differ in their penchant for fanaticism. If there are no finite upper or lower bounds on the value of outcomes, then MEV implies Narrow Fanaticism (and any other natural formalization of fanaticism). And if moral value does have a privileged cardinal structure, it seems very plausible that it should be unbounded: For instance, if adding a happy or unhappy life to the world makes a contribution to its overall value that depends only on the intrinsic characteristics of that life, and if there is no upper bound on the number of lives (of a particular intrinsic character) that the world might contain, then value is unbounded.

MEU, on the other hand, allows both fanatical and nonfanatical preferences.[15] An agent's utility function might simply be a linear function of moral value. But it might also dampen MEV's fanaticism, by being concave (risk-averse) with respect to sufficiently good outcomes and convex (risk-seeking) with respect to sufficiently bad outcomes. More particularly, even if value is unbounded, and an agent's utility function is an increasing function of value, her utilities can still be bounded (see Figure 1).[16] In this case, low-probability

---

[15] Thus, if the *only* requirements on rational preference are those stated by MEU (perhaps combined with a requirement to prefer better outcomes to worse outcomes), then a form of permissivism would be true. But MEU is compatible with the existence of further, more constraining rational requirements.

[16] Certain axiomatizations of expected utility theory *require* that utility is bounded, thereby ruling out fanaticism. But it's also possible to axiomatize expected utility in ways that permit unbounded utilities. See fn. 45 for discussion.

outcomes will carry only limited weight in her decisions, no matter how astronomically good or bad they are.

## 3 The Case for Fanaticism

We turn now to our central task, namely considering the arguments for and against both fanaticism and anti-fanaticism. In this section and the next, we will focus on fanaticism. Various arguments for fanaticism have been made in the recent literature.[17] In this section I will discuss two such arguments, focusing primarily on the second, which I take to be the most compelling (although, as I will explain, I am ultimately unpersuaded by it).

### 3.1 The Spectrum Argument

Let's begin with the *simplest* argument for fanaticism. Focusing on positive fanaticism (here as elsewhere, the negative and positive cases are exactly formally analogous), the essence of this argument is that we can get from certainty of a good outcome ($\langle o^+ \rangle$) to a tiny probability of an astronomically good outcome coupled with near-certainty of a bad outcome ($\langle o^{*+}, p, o^- \rangle$) by a series of small steps each of which seems intuitively like an improvement.[18] The argument relies on two principles. The first says, roughly, that one should always be willing to accept *a very slight* decrease in the probability of a desired outcome in exchange for a sufficiently great increase in its desirability.

**Non-Timidity** It is rationally required that there is some $q < 1$ such that, for any outcomes $o^+ >_0 o^-$ and probability $p > 0$, there is an outcome $o^{++}$ such that $\langle o^{++}, q'p, o^- \rangle > \langle o^+, p, o^- \rangle$ for any $q' \geq q$.

Suppose, for instance, that you are facing a risky medical procedure, and can choose between two options: a "safe" option that maximizes your probability of surviving the procedure, and a "risky" option that will improve your quality of life if you do survive. Non-Timidity says that if the difference in your chance of survival is sufficiently small, and the difference in quality of life sufficiently great, then you should take the risky option.

The second principle says that an agent's ranking of prospects should be *transitive*.

---

<sup></sup>[17] Wilkinson (2022) offers the most full-throated defense of fanaticism, giving three distinct arguments. Russell (2023) and Beckstead and Thomas (2024) discuss arguments both for and against fanaticism, without reaching a firm conclusion. Kowalczyk (forthcoming) defends a limited form of fanaticism.

[18] A version of this argument first appears in Beckstead (2013, Ch. 6), and it is further developed in Wilkinson (2022) and Beckstead and Thomas (2024).

**Transitivity** It is rationally required that, if $P_i$ is weakly preferred to $P_j$ and $P_j$ is weakly preferred to $P_k$, then $P_i$ is weakly preferred to $P_k$.

Transitivity is a very widely accepted principle in normative decision theory. Many find it simply incoherent that you should prefer a first thing to a second, and a second to a third, but fail to prefer the first to the third. And Transitivity can also be supported by dynamic consistency arguments (see for instance Gustafsson, 2022, §4). It is far from uncontroversial, but entering into those controversies is beyond the scope of this work, so I will mostly take Transitivity for granted.

It is fairly easy to see that Non-Timidity and Transitivity together entail Narrow Positive Fanaticism: For any $o^+$ and $o^-$, we can start from certainty of $o^+$ (i.e., $\langle o^+, 1, o^- \rangle$) and work our way to a prospect of the form $\langle o^{*+}, p', o^- \rangle$ by a series of improving steps, each time improving the more desirable outcome of the prospect while slightly reducing its probability by multiplying it by a factor of $q$ or greater. And if each prospect in this sequence is strictly preferred to the one before, then the long shot at the end of the sequence must be strictly preferred to the safe bet we started off with.[19] Call this the *Spectrum Argument* for fanaticism.

This argument rests on an appeal to intuition: the intuition of Non-Timidity, that one should be willing to accept *some* extra risk in exchange for a sufficiently great increase in reward. The opponent of fanaticism can always deny this intuition (Bottomley and Williamson, 2025, fn. 18) – or, less plausibly in my opinion, deny Transitivity. But the force of the argument is to weaken any presumption *against* fanaticism on the basis of intuition. We saw in the last section that fanaticism can be deeply counterintuitive. We now see that *avoiding* fanaticism also requires an agent to exhibit strange and counterintuitive preferences, whether by violating Non-Timidity or Transitivity.

## 3.2  More Setup: Outcomes as Populations

My main focus, however, will be on an argument for fanaticism that's more complicated but also, I think, more compelling. This argument is couched in a formal framework for representing outcomes which we must first introduce. In this framework, the value of an outcome is determined by "local outcomes" realized at distinct "value locations." These concepts can be interpreted in various ways. In a prudential context, for instance, "locations" could be identified with moments in an individual's life, and "local outcomes" with possible states

---

[19] This relies on the fact that transitivity of weak preference, the principle stated in the main text, entails transitivity of strict preference (the requirement that, if $P_i > P_j$ and $P_j > P_k$, then $P_i > P_k$).

(e.g., experiential states) that an individual might be in at a particular moment. But the most common interpretation of the framework of locations, and the one that will make the following argument most compelling, is ethical. On this interpretation, locations are identified with welfare subjects (beings with morally significant welfare interests) and local outcomes with welfare states (specifications of all the features of an individual's life that influence her welfare, like how long it lasts and what experiences it includes). I will informally assume this interpretation, and so use "welfare subject" or "individual" interchangeably with "value location," and "welfare state" or "life" interchangeably with "local outcome." But the formal arguments we consider won't depend on this interpretation.

Our first task, then, is to set out a formal framework for describing outcomes in terms of local outcomes realized at locations. So, let $\mathcal{L}$ be an infinite set of possible locations, and let $\mathcal{W}$ be a set of local outcomes, including an element $\omega$ representing nonexistence. Local outcomes are ranked by a total preorder $\succeq_{\mathcal{W}}$, where $w_i \succeq_{\mathcal{W}} w_j$ means that $w_i$ is at least as good as $w_j$. An *outcome* can now be understood as a function $o : \mathcal{L} \to \mathcal{W}$ specifying local outcomes for each location (and thereby specifying, among other things, which locations exist). Any prospect $P$ then defines a *local prospect $P^l$* for each location $l$, a probability distribution over local outcomes.

As always, we will restrict our attention to finite outcomes, meaning here outcomes in which all but finitely many locations are assigned nonexistence. And we will continue to assume, implicitly, that the domain $\mathbb{P}$ of prospects includes at least all finitely supported probability distributions over these finite outcomes. At some points below, however, we'll explicitly make the following stronger assumption:

**Full Domain** The set of prospects $\mathbb{P}$ includes all discrete probability measures on $\mathbb{O}$, including those that assign non-zero probability to a countable infinity of outcomes.

## 3.3 The Argument from Anteriority

We can now develop a second, and in my opinion more compelling, argument for fanaticism.[20] The argument rests on two central ideas. The first is a kind of "individualism": Our basic objects of concern should be individual value locations, rather than the world as a whole. Prospects, therefore, should be compared "from the perspective of" each value location. (I'll use "from the

---

[20] The following argument combines features of the separability-based arguments discussed in Wilkinson (2022, 2024), Russell (2023), and Beckstead and Thomas (2024) and the argument in Kowalczyk (forthcoming) from *ex ante* Pareto and the "Better-Chance Principle."

perspective of" as shorthand for "considering only the interests of"; the talk of "perspectives" shouldn't be taken literally.) If one prospect is better than another from the perspective of some locations, but worse from the perspective of others, then we must make tradeoffs between different locations. But if one prospect is better than another from the perspective of every location, then it is better overall; and if two prospects are equally good from the perspective of every location, then they are equally good overall. These claims are, of course, particularly plausible if we are identifying value locations with welfare subjects.

One apparent implication of this individualist stance is the following principle:

**Anteriority (McCarthy et al., 2020)**  If for each possible value location $l$, $P_i$ and $P_j$ give the same probability distribution over local outcomes (i.e., $P_i^l = P_j^l$ for all $l \in \mathcal{L}$), then it is rationally required that $P_i \sim P_j$.

This follows from two arguably more basic principles:

***Ex Ante* Pareto Indifference**  If $P_i$ and $P_j$ are equally good from the perspective of every location, then it is rationally required that $P_i \sim P_j$.

**Individual Stochasticism**  If $P_i$ and $P_j$ give $l$ the same probability distribution over local outcomes, then they are equally good from $l$'s perspective.

The second central idea is that there is a generic, repeatable way of making outcomes better or worse, that is always capable of "bridging the gap" between a better outcome and a worse outcome. This generic method could take either of two forms: changing the welfare of an existing individual, or adding new individuals. I will focus on the latter. The idea that we can always bridge the gap between better and worse outcomes by adding individuals to either outcome is precisified by the following principles:

**Positive Additions**  For any outcomes $o^+$ and $o^-$, there is a number $n$ and a welfare level $w^+$ such that adding $n$ or more individuals with welfare $w^+$ to outcome $o^-$, while leaving everything else unchanged, results in an outcome strictly better than $o^+$ (regardless of the identities of the added individuals).

**Negative Additions**  For any outcomes $o^+$ and $o^-$, there is a number $n$ and a welfare level $w^-$ such that adding $n$ or more individuals with welfare $w^-$ to outcome $o^+$, while leaving everything else unchanged, results in an outcome strictly worse than $o^-$ (regardless of the identities of the added individuals).

These principles will be rejected by those like Bader (2022), who hold that populations of different sizes are always incomparable in overall value. Positive

Additions will also be rejected by those who hold that some forms of suffering cannot be outweighed by any amount of positive welfare. But a very wide range of axiologies endorse both principles, including not just additive views like total utilitarianism, critical-level utilitarianism, and prioritarianism but also views like "variable-value utilitarianism" (Hurka, 1983) which treat additions to a population as having sharply diminishing marginal value.[21]

The argument for fanaticism will need two more apparently innocuous principles. One is Transitivity, introduced above. The other is a very weak dominance principle.

**Superdominance** If every possible outcome of $P_i$ is strictly better than every possible outcome of $P_j$, then it is rationally required that $P_i$ is strictly preferred to $P_j$.

Superdominance is among the weakest and least controversial principles of normative decision theory. It seems to follow self-evidently from the idea that we should evaluate an uncertain prospect based on the desirability of its possible outcomes. We will shortly find a surprising reason to question this principle, but for now, let's take it on board.

Here, then, is the promised argument for fanaticism, which in light of its central premise we will call the *Argument from Anteriority*:

**Proposition 1** *Anteriority, Superdominance, Transitivity, and Positive Additions together imply Narrow Positive Fanaticism. Likewise, Anteriority, Superdominance, Transitivity, and Negative Additions together imply Narrow Negative Fanaticism.*[22]

*Proof* As usual, let's focus on the positive case (the negative case being exactly parallel). Consider, then, two arbitrary outcomes $o^+ \succ_0 o^-$ and an arbitrary probability $p > 0$. Our goal is to find an outcome $o^{*+}$ such that $\langle o^{*+}, p', o^- \rangle$ is strictly preferred to $\langle o^+ \rangle$ for all $p' \geq p$. We will do this as follows: First, we choose an $m$ large enough that $\frac{1}{m} \leq p$. Next, by Positive Additions, there is

---

[21] Even average utilitarianism implies Positive and Negative Additions, as long as there is no maximum or minimum possible welfare level (which does not imply that individual welfare is in any sense unbounded): If we add enough lives to $o^-$ with welfare greater than the average welfare in $o^+$, for instance, the resulting average will eventually exceed that of $o^+$.

[22] The same premises also imply a stronger form of fanaticism, symmetric to the thesis of General Anti-Fanaticism introduced in Section 6. One can also prove a very similar result that replaces Positive/Negative Additions with principles asserting that, for any $o^+$ and $o^-$, we can get an outcome better than $o^+$ by improving the welfare of any one individual in $o^-$, and an outcome worse than $o^-$ by worsening the welfare of any one individual in $o^+$. This result requires a somewhat stronger dominance principle than Superdominance, though, and the assumption that at least two individuals exist in $o^+/o^-$.

**Table 1** Illustration of the Argument from Anteriority. $\text{Pop}(o^-)$ is the set of individuals who exist in $o^-$ and $\text{Dist}(o^-)$ represents their welfare distribution in $o^-$.

### (A) Prospect $P^\uparrow$

| | $s_0\ (p'')$ | $s_1\left(\frac{1-p''}{m}\right)$ | $s_2\left(\frac{1-p''}{m}\right)$ | $\cdots$ | $s_m\left(\frac{1-p''}{m}\right)$ |
|---|---|---|---|---|---|
| $\text{Pop}(o^-)$ | $\text{Dist}(o^-)$ | $\text{Dist}(o^-)$ | $\text{Dist}(o^-)$ | $\cdots$ | $\text{Dist}(o^-)$ |
| $p_1-p_n$ | $w^+$ | $w^+$ | — | $\cdots$ | — |
| $p_{n+1}-p_{2n}$ | $w^+$ | — | $w^+$ | $\cdots$ | — |
| $\vdots$ | $\vdots$ | $\vdots$ | $\vdots$ | $\ddots$ | $\vdots$ |
| $p_{n(m-1)+1}-p_{nm}$ | $w^+$ | — | — | $\cdots$ | $w^+$ |

### (B) Prospect $P^*$

| | $s_0\ (p'')$ | $s_1\left(\frac{1-p''}{m}\right)$ | $s_2\left(\frac{1-p''}{m}\right)$ | $\cdots$ | $s_m\left(\frac{1-p''}{m}\right)$ |
|---|---|---|---|---|---|
| $\text{Pop}(o^-)$ | $\text{Dist}(o^-)$ | $\text{Dist}(o^-)$ | $\text{Dist}(o^-)$ | $\cdots$ | $\text{Dist}(o^-)$ |
| $p_1-p_n$ | $w^+$ | $w^+$ | — | $\cdots$ | — |
| $p_{n+1}-p_{2n}$ | $w^+$ | $w^+$ | — | $\cdots$ | — |
| $\vdots$ | $\vdots$ | $\vdots$ | $\vdots$ | $\ddots$ | $\vdots$ |
| $p_{n(m-1)+1}-p_{nm}$ | $w^+$ | $w^+$ | — | $\cdots$ | — |

an $n$ and a $w^+$ such that adding $n$ or more individuals with welfare $w^+$ to $o^-$ yields an outcome better than $o^+$. We will show that an outcome that adds $n \times m$ individuals with welfare $w^+$ to $o^-$ has the properties required of $o^{*+}$.

To do this, we consider an arbitrary $p' \geq p$. We define $p'' = (mp'-1)/(m-1)$. (Since $p' \geq p \geq \frac{1}{m}$, $p''$ is guaranteed to be non-negative.) We then consider a prospect $P^\uparrow$ that, in each of $m$ equiprobable states $s_1-s_m$, each with probability $\frac{1-p''}{m}$, yields $o^-$ combined with $n$ added individuals with welfare $w^+$, with a *different* set of individuals added in each state; and, in a further state $s_0$ with probability $p''$, yields $o^-$ together with *all* of these possible individuals, still with welfare $w^+$. This prospect is illustrated in Table 1a. Since by Positive Additions every possible outcome of $P^\uparrow$ is better than $o^+$, Superdominance requires that $P^\uparrow$ be strictly preferred to $\langle o^+ \rangle$.

The next step is to permute the local prospects of each group of added individuals, other than the first, so that they all exist with welfare $w^+$ in states $s_0$ and $s_1$ and don't exist in any other states. The resulting prospect $P^*$ is illustrated in Table 1b. Since permuting outcomes between equally probable states doesn't change any individual's probability of achieving any given welfare level, Anteriority implies that $P^*$ must be preferred equally with $P^\uparrow$. Since $P^* \sim P^\uparrow > \langle o^+ \rangle$, Transitivity requires that $P^* > \langle o^+ \rangle$. We have thus found an outcome $o^{*+}$ such that, for any $p' \geq p$, the prospect $\langle o^{*+}, p', o^- \rangle$ is strictly preferred to $\langle o^+ \rangle$, as required. $\qquad\square$

## 3.4 An Infinitary Puzzle

But there's a problem for this argument: in certain infinitary contexts, the principles to which we appealed in support of fanaticism turn out to be inconsistent!

**Proposition 2** *Given Full Domain, the principles of Anteriority, Positive and Negative Additions, and Superdominance are mutually inconsistent.*

*Proof* We can use Positive and Negative Additions to construct a pair of prospects $P^+$ and $P^-$ that must be preferred equally by Anteriority, but where the former must be strictly preferred to the latter by Superdominance. We do this as follows.[23] First, we consider a set of states with probabilities $\frac{1}{2}, \frac{1}{4}, \frac{1}{8}$, and so on, and an arbitrary "baseline" outcome $o_b$. We then find welfare levels $w_1^+$ and $w_1^-$ and a number $n$ such that adding $n$ lives with welfare $w_1^+$ to $o_b$ results in an outcome $o_1^+$ strictly better than $o_b$, and adding $n$ lives with welfare $w_1^-$ to $o_b$ results in an outcome $o_1^-$ strictly worse than $o_b$. (Positive and Negative Additions guarantee that this is possible.) We then choose an initial group of $n$ individuals, who will exist in every state in both prospects. In $P^+$, these individuals receive $w_1^+$ in state $s_1$ and $w_1^-$ in all remaining states, while in $P^-$ this is reversed: they receive $w_1^-$ in state $s_1$ and $w_1^+$ in all remaining states. Under both prospects, however, they are certain to exist and have equal probabilities of receiving $w_1^+$ or $w_1^-$ conditional on existence.

Next, we do something similar in state $s_2$: We find new welfare levels $w_2^+$ and $w_2^-$ and a number $m$ such that adding $m$ individuals with welfare $w_2^+$ to $o_1^-$ results in an outcome $o_2^+$ that's strictly better than $o_b$, and likewise adding $m$ individuals with welfare $w_2^-$ to $o_1^+$ results in an outcome $o_2^-$ that's strictly worse than $o_b$. Again, Positive and Negative Additions guarantee that this is possible. We then choose a second group of $m$ individuals, who will exist in every state but $s_1$ in both prospects. In $P^+$, these individuals receive $w_2^+$ in state $s_2$ and $w_2^-$ in all subsequent states, while in $P^-$, they receive $w_2^-$ in state $s_2$ and $w_2^+$ in all subsequent states. Again, both prospects give them the same probability of existence, and equal probabilities of $w_2^+$ or $w_2^-$ conditional on existence.

---

[23] The following example combines elements from related examples in Goodsell (2021), Kowalczyk (forthcoming), and Tarsney et al. (2025).

**Table 2** An illustration of the conflict between Anteriority, Superdominance, and Positive/Negative Additions. Each individual has the same probability of existing in both prospects (with " —" representing nonexistence), and equal probabilities of a positive and a negative welfare level conditional on existence. But every outcome of $P^+$ is strictly better than the baseline outcome $o_b$, while every outcome of $P^-$ is strictly worse.

### (A) $P^+$: Surely Better than Baseline

| | $s_1\left(\frac{1}{2}\right)$ | $s_2\left(\frac{1}{4}\right)$ | $s_3\left(\frac{1}{8}\right)$ | $s_4\left(\frac{1}{16}\right)$ | $\cdots$ |
|---|---|---|---|---|---|
| Pop($o_b$) | Dist($o_b$) | Dist($o_b$) | Dist($o_b$) | Dist($o_b$) | $\cdots$ |
| 1st Addition | $w_1^+$ | $w_1^-$ | $w_1^-$ | $w_1^-$ | $\cdots$ |
| 2nd Addition | — | $w_2^+$ | $w_2^-$ | $w_2^-$ | $\cdots$ |
| 3rd Addition | — | — | $w_3^+$ | $w_3^-$ | $\cdots$ |
| 4th Addition | — | — | — | $w_4^+$ | $\cdots$ |
| $\vdots$ | $\vdots$ | $\vdots$ | $\vdots$ | $\vdots$ | $\ddots$ |

### (B) $P^-$: Surely Worse than Baseline

| | $s_1\left(\frac{1}{2}\right)$ | $s_2\left(\frac{1}{4}\right)$ | $s_3\left(\frac{1}{8}\right)$ | $s_4\left(\frac{1}{16}\right)$ | $\cdots$ |
|---|---|---|---|---|---|
| Pop($o_b$) | Dist($o_b$) | Dist($o_b$) | Dist($o_b$) | Dist($o_b$) | $\cdots$ |
| 1st Addition | $w_1^-$ | $w_1^+$ | $w_1^+$ | $w_1^+$ | $\cdots$ |
| 2nd Addition | — | $w_2^-$ | $w_2^+$ | $w_2^+$ | $\cdots$ |
| 3rd Addition | — | — | $w_3^-$ | $w_3^+$ | $\cdots$ |
| 4th Addition | — | — | — | $w_4^-$ | $\cdots$ |
| $\vdots$ | $\vdots$ | $\vdots$ | $\vdots$ | $\vdots$ | $\ddots$ |

Continuing this process *ad infinitum* gives us the prospects $P^+$ and $P^-$ shown in Table 2. On the one hand, every possible outcome of $P^+$ is strictly better than $o_b$, and every possible outcome of $P^-$ is strictly worse than $o_b$. Thus, every possible outcome of $P^+$ is strictly better than every possible outcome of $P^-$. (Here we are using the assumption from Section 2.1 that the betterness relation on outcomes is transitive.) So by Superdominance, it is required that $P^+ > P^-$. On the other hand, for each possible individual, $P^+$ and $P^-$ give the same probability distribution over local outcomes (including nonexistence). So Anteriority requires that $P^+ \sim P^-$.      $\square$

This isn't just an isolated problem with the particular set of premises we chose when making the case for fanaticism. It reflects a basic tension, in infinitary contexts, between "localist" principles (like Anteriority) that evaluate prospects from the perspective of particular locations or sets of locations considered in isolation and "universalist" principles (like Superdominance) that evaluate prospects by looking at the overall value of their possible outcomes.[24] And it is likely to afflict any argument for fanaticism that relies on principles of both types. In particular, Russell (2023) and Kowalczyk (forthcoming) both show that pro-fanatical arguments conceptually related to the Anteriority-based argument we've been discussing run into exactly the same sort of trouble: the premises that imply fanaticism in a finitary context turn out to be inconsistent in an infinitary context.

## 3.5 Against Anteriority

This doesn't necessarily mean that the Anteriority-based argument for fanaticism fails. That argument only relied on strictly finite applications of the various principles involved. And so it can be rescued from inconsistency either by restricting our domain (denying that infinitary prospects like $P^+$ and $P^-$ are even possible) or, more plausibly, restricting the scope of one or more of its premises. In particular, we might restrict either Anteriority or Superdominance so that they only apply to prospects with finitely many possible outcomes.[25] This would require some sacrifice of intuition – after all, both these principles seem very plausible in their unrestricted forms, and the need to deny either of them in any context is counterintuitive. But infinities are counterintuitive in lots of ways, and many intuitive generalizations turn out to be true in finite contexts but false in infinite contexts. If we take this line, then the case for fanaticism is still going strong.

On the other hand, we might think that the need to give up either Anteriority or Superdominance in infinite contexts is telling us that one of those principles, despite its appeal, rests on a mistake. If the basic thoughts that motivated those principles do not distinguish between finite and infinite contexts, then we cannot restrict either principle without giving up its basic motivation; and once we have done that, we should no longer feel particularly attached to its finite rump. On this view, infinitary inconsistency results like the one above undercut the case for fanaticism.

---

[24] This tension is illustrated by various impossibility results in the recent literature, from Goodsell (2021), Wilkinson (2023), Russell (2023), Kowalczyk (forthcoming), Hong and Russell (2025), and Tarsney et al. (2025).

[25] The other principles on which Proposition 2 depends, namely Positive/Negative Additions and the transitivity of $\succsim_O$, concern outcomes not prospects, so no analogous restriction can be applied to them.

I favor the latter response, though for somewhat idiosyncratic reasons. I will conclude this section by setting out those reasons, though I don't expect them to convince everyone.

To my mind, the conflict between "individualist"/"localist" and "universalist" principles in infinite contexts indicates that we must make a fundamental choice between these two ways of evaluating prospects: focusing either on the perspective of each individual location, or on the overall value of each possible outcome. And it is the individualist perspective that rests on a mistake. The mistake is not in thinking that individuals are the fundamental bearers of value, or that our fundamental concern should be with their welfare. Rather, the mistake is in thinking that there is a morally privileged way of "matching up" individuals across different possible outcomes (a transworld identity or counterpart relation) that allows us to *compare* different outcomes or prospects from the perspective of one and the same individual. I'm skeptical that any such relation is metaphysically substantial enough to bear moral weight: I don't know what it means, for instance, to ask whether some individual in a different possible world or a counterfactual scenario would be "identical with" some actual individual, and I don't see how any "counterpart" relation between individuals in different possible worlds could be anything other than an arbitrary human creation (even if it is a great conceptual convenience in many contexts). But individualistic principles like Anteriority fundamentally depend on such identifications, since their application requires us to compare the welfare of the same individual, or counterpart individuals, across different outcomes.[26]

Without such identifications, the truth that individuals are the fundamental loci of value leads in a different direction: The *absolute* value of an outcome is grounded in the welfare of each particular individual who exists in that outcome. But the *comparative* value of two different outcomes is grounded not in an individual-by-individual comparison (which would require a privileged way of matching up individuals), but in the absolute values of each outcome. Likewise, the comparative rational desirability of two *prospects* is grounded not in an individual-by-individual comparison of local prospects, but in the absolute desirability of each prospect, which is grounded in the absolute values and probabilities of its various possible outcomes. Thus, the fact that the interests of individuals are what fundamentally matter (and *ultimately* ground the comparative value of outcomes and prospects) doesn't imply that we must compare

---

[26] For related worries about *ex ante* Pareto-style principles, based on the difficulties of nonarbitrarily matching up individuals across possible worlds, see Mahtani (2017, 2024).

outcomes and prospects "from the perspective of" each possible individual. The appeal of principles like Anteriority rests on the natural but mistaken belief in the meaningfulness of cross-world identifications.

This picture supports an unrestricted version of Superdominance and, I will later argue, of stronger dominance principles as well. And while it does not rule out that Anteriority or similar principles might hold true at least in finite contexts, it undercuts our justification for believing them.

But there is also positive reason to doubt Anteriority in finite contexts. For instance, consider the following example:

**Great Escape** Humanity has just learned, much to our collective chagrin, that all life on Earth will be inevitably wiped out in just fifty years: An intermediate-mass black hole is headed our way on a trajectory that will take it through the inner Solar System, either swallowing Earth or ejecting it into interstellar space. Our only hope for the long-term survival of humanity is to rapidly build an interstellar spacecraft that will let a few individuals escape to another star system and start over. There are two candidate designs for the drive system of this spacecraft, either of which would require such an investment of resources that it's not possible to build both. Unfortunately, which design will allow us to successfully reach and settle another system depends on still-unresolved questions in fundamental physics: If Theory 1 is correct, then only Design 1 will be successful, while if Theory 2 is correct, only Design 2 will be successful. Scientists regard these two theories as equally likely. As it turns out, the theories also have distinctive cosmological implications. Theory 1 implies that the universe as a whole is very large (many, many orders of magnitude larger than the observable universe), so large that it almost certainly contains millions of other intelligent civilizations – though so far away that we will almost certainly never come in contact with them. Theory 2 implies that the universe is relatively small (not much larger than the observable universe), in which case – we now believe – humanity's existence was a lucky fluke, and it is extremely unlikely that there is or will be intelligent life anywhere else in the universe.

The choice of which drive system to build, we can stipulate, makes no difference to any individual's probability of ending up with a given individual outcome. The same individuals will be chosen to crew the spacecraft either way, and while the choice might affect which future individuals are born, we have no ex ante knowledge of those effects, and cannot say that any particular individual is more likely to be born or more likely to achieve a given welfare level if we choose one design rather than the other. Nevertheless, in light of the cosmological implications of the two theories, it strikes me as entirely reasonable to strictly prefer Design 2: In choosing Design 1, we run an especially great risk, for if Theory 2 turns out to be true, then we will be left with a universe forever more devoid of life and intelligence, and in which those things only ever existed as a tiny, ephemeral flicker. In choosing Design 2, we greatly reduce that risk, for it is very likely that *either* humanity will survive and flourish (if Theory 2 is correct) *or* other civilizations, elsewhere in the universe will do so (if Theory 1 is correct). That seems like a sufficient justification for preferring Design 2. It would even be rationally permissible, I think, to prefer and to choose Design 2 if it came at some significant extra cost (e.g., requiring a small additional tax on every member of the present population).

This case provides not just a motivation for rejecting Anteriority but one that is particularly germane to the question of fanaticism. What the case illustrates is that it is prima facie reasonable to have non-neutral risk attitudes toward the overall value of outcomes, like wanting to maximize the probability that the world achieves some threshold of value (e.g., the threshold corresponding to a long-lived, flourishing civilization). These risk attitudes are exactly what supply our intuitions against fanaticism: in both prudential and moral decision-making contexts, we are often driven by goals like maximizing the probability of a "good enough" outcome or minimizing the probability of a "catastrophic" outcome.[27] These concerns with particular thresholds make us sensitive to *correlations* between individual prospects – correlations which Anteriority tells us to ignore (as, for instance, when it tells us that $P^\uparrow$ and $P^*$ are equally good, in the argument for fanaticism from Section 3.3). If Anteriority is well-motivated (in particular, by the idea that we must compare prospects by comparing them from the point of view of each individual), then it shows us that these concerns are irrational. But if those motivations are undercut, then we should stick with our judgment that threshold concerns of the sort illustrated by The Great Escape are reasonable and rational.[28]

---

[27]  Bottomley and Williamson (2025, 324) make a similar point in answering a different argument for fanaticism.

[28]  Similar considerations undercut arguments for fanaticism based on Prospect Separability that have been widely discussed in the recent literature (see note 20). Roughly, Prospect Separability asserts that if the choice between two prospects only affects some subset of the population, the ranking of those prospects can be determined just by looking at the affected part of the population, without reference to the unaffected part. The intuition in favor of Drive 2 in Great Escape, and other examples of intuitive risk aversion with respect to overall value, count against Prospect Separability as well as Anteriority. And the strongest motivations for Prospect Separability, in my opinion, appeal to Anteriority or closely related "individualist" principles, so undercutting the motivation for Anteriority undercuts the motivation for Prospect Separability as well.

## 4 The Case against Fanaticism

We've now seen that there is a strong argument to be made for fanaticism – though one by which I at least am ultimately unpersuaded. In this chapter, we'll see that there is also a strong argument to be made *against* fanaticism.

The *simplest* argument against fanaticism, of course, is just that it's deeply counterintuitive. Is it really plausible that we're *required* to give up certainty of a utopian future for the near-certainty of a hellish future, coupled with a $10^{-100}$ chance of the right super-utopian future? We shouldn't wholly discount these intuitions in favor of formal arguments – if nothing else, they place a burden of justification on the fanatic that cannot be met, for instance, just by claiming that the correctness of expected value maximization is intuitively obvious.

But we can also give a more principled reason for opposing fanaticism.

### 4.1 Generalized St. Petersburg Prospects

The St. Petersburg lottery is a game in which a fair coin is flipped repeatedly until it lands tails. The player then receives a payoff of $\$2^n$, where $n$ is the total number of flips. What is interesting about this game is that, because the player wins \$2 with probability $\frac{1}{2}$, \$4 with probability $\frac{1}{4}$, \$8 with probability $\frac{1}{8}$, and so on, the *expected* monetary reward from playing the game (the probability-weighted sum of its possible monetary payoffs) is infinite: $\$1 + \$1 + \$1 + \dots$. A gambler who aims to maximize their expected wealth, therefore, should be willing to pay any finite price for a St. Petersburg lottery ticket. What makes this conclusion especially puzzling is that every possible payoff of the game is finite. Thus, expectational reasoning appears to tell us that the St. Petersburg game is worth more than *any* of its possible payoffs.

The classic response to this puzzle, in its original formulation, is to point out that money has diminishing marginal utility: the richer you are, the less you benefit from one more dollar. And the rational way to evaluate monetary gambles is by expected *utility*, not expected *monetary reward*. (Thus, for instance, anyone who is not already very rich should prefer certainty of \$1 million to a 1% chance of \$101 million.) Given a realistically concave function from money to utility, the St. Petersburg game has only finite expected utility.[29]

But this response by itself doesn't resolve the basic decision-theoretic paradox. For as long as an expected utility maximizer's function from wealth to utility has no upper bound, we can find a St. Petersburg-like gamble with infinite expected *utility*, to which she must apparently assign infinite value (Menger, 1934). We can again imagine a fair coin flipped until it lands tails, and construct

---

[29] The *locus classicus* for this response to the paradox is Bernoulli (1738).

a prospect where if the coin lands tails on the first flip, the agent receives a monetary payoff with utility $x$ (or greater), if it lands tails on the second flip, she receives a monetary payoff with utility $2x$ (or greater), $4x$ on the third flip, $8x$ on the fourth flip, and so on. Thus, in the context of expected utility theory, the St. Petersburg game has often been taken to show that utility functions must be bounded.[30]

But the St. Petersburg paradox isn't confined to expected utility theory. It turns out that Narrow Fanaticism, with modest auxiliary assumptions, implies that we can construct "Generalized St. Petersburg prospects" with the same paradoxical features as the original – specifically, prospects that are "improper" in that they must be strictly preferred, or strictly dispreferred, to any of their possible outcomes.[31] Here's how we do it (focusing, as usual, on the positive case): Take two arbitrary outcomes $o^+$ and $o^-$, with $o^+$ strictly better than $o^-$. Narrow Fanaticism implies that there is an outcome $o_1$ such that $\langle o_1, \frac{1}{2}, o^- \rangle$ is strictly preferred to $\langle o^+ \rangle$; an outcome $o_2$ such that $\langle o_2, \frac{1}{4}, o^- \rangle$ is strictly preferred to $\langle o_1 \rangle$; an outcome $o_3$ such that $\langle o_3, \frac{1}{8}, o^- \rangle$ is strictly preferred to $\langle o_2 \rangle$; and so on. Now, consider the following prospect:

**Generalized St. Petersburg** A fair coin is flipped until it lands tails, yielding the outcome $o_n$, where $n$ is the total number of flips. This generates the prospect $\langle (o_1, \frac{1}{2}), (o_2, \frac{1}{4}), (o_3, \frac{1}{8}), \ldots \rangle$.

To show that Generalized St. Petersburg is strictly preferable to each of its possible outcomes (or, strictly speaking, to the prospects that yield those outcomes with certainty), we need one new principle.

**Stochastic Dominance** If for any outcome $o$, $P_i$ is at least as likely as $P_j$ to yield an outcome at least as good as $o$, then it is rationally required that $P_i \succsim P_j$. If in addition, for some outcome $o$, $P_i$ is strictly more likely than $P_j$ to yield an outcome at least as good as $o$, then it is rationally required that $P_i \succ P_j$.

When the first of the above conditions is met, we say that $P_i$ *weakly stochastically dominates* $P_j$. When the second condition is also met, we say that $P_i$ *strictly stochastically dominates* $P_j$.

Though it is substantially stronger than the principle of Superdominance we relied on in the last section, Stochastic Dominance is still one of the least

---

[30] See for instance Arrow (1951, 425; 1974, 64–65), Savage (1972, 80–82), Aumann (1977), Bassett (1987), Joyce (1999, 38). For more on the St. Petersburg game and the decision-theoretic lessons that have been drawn from it, see Peterson (2023).

[31] Versions of the following arguments are discussed in Russell and Isaacs (2021), Russell (2023), and Beckstead and Thomas (2024). The term "improper prospects" is due to Russell and Isaacs (2021).

controversial principles in normative decision theory.[32] Various arguments can be made in its favor. But the most compelling argument, to my mind, appeals to the idea that what ultimately matters in evaluating prospects, and gives us reason to form particular preferences between them, are the values and probabilities of their potential outcomes. When $P_i$ and $P_j$ offer the same probabilities of achieving any given level of value, then there is no evaluatively significant consideration favoring either prospect, and the only rationally appropriate attitude is indifference. When $P_i$ strictly stochastically dominates $P_j$, there is a contrastive consideration in favor of $P_i$ (there is some threshold or "aspiration level" of value that it gives you a better chance of achieving), but no contrastive consideration in favor of $P_j$: for any outcome one might point to as an inducement to choose $P_j$, $P_i$ is at least as likely to yield an outcome at least that good. And these seem like decisive grounds for preferring $P_i$.[33]

Stochastic Dominance and Transitivity together imply that Generalized St. Petersburg is strictly preferable to $\langle o_n \rangle$, for each of its possible outcomes $o_n$. Narrow (Positive) Fanaticism allowed us to stipulate that, for every $n$, the prospect $\langle o_{n+1}, \frac{1}{2^{n+1}}, o^- \rangle$ is strictly preferred to $\langle o_n \rangle$. By Stochastic Dominance, Generalized St. Petersburg is strictly preferred to $\langle o_{n+1}, \frac{1}{2^{n+1}}, o^- \rangle$ (since it has the same probability of yielding outcome $o_{n+1}$, and all its other possible outcomes are strictly better than $o^-$). So, by Transitivity, Generalized St. Petersburg is strictly preferred to $\langle o_n \rangle$, for every $n$.

## 4.2 Money-Pumping Fanatics

The existence of prospects like Generalized St. Petersburg is not just odd, but has a number of seriously undesirable consequences. In particular, an agent who strictly prefers (or disprefers) some prospect to all its possible outcomes will, given plausible principles of sequential choice, sometimes make sequences of choices that are certainly worse than available alternatives.

---

[32] In particular, given the requirement that certainty of a better outcome be strictly preferred to certainty of a worse outcome, Stochastic Dominance is implied not only by expected utility theory but by various alternative decision theories that permit a wider range of risk attitudes, like risk-weighted expected utility (Buchak, 2013) and the version of weighted-linear utility theory defended by Bottomley and Williamson (2024). The principle is not entirely uncontroversial, though. It has been challenged in contexts involving incomparable outcomes (Bales et al., 2014; Schoenfield, 2014) and, more relevant for our purposes, in contexts involving St. Petersburg-like gambles (Seidenfeld et al., 2009). Space constraints preclude a full discussion of these challenges, but see Bader (2018) and Meacham (2019) for replies to the former and latter challenges respectively. Finally, the characterization of stochastic dominance requires some revision in contexts where the evaluative ordering of outcomes is incomplete or has certain exotic infinitary structures – see Russell (forthcoming). But these extra complications won't matter for our purposes.

[33] An argument along these lines for the verdict of Stochastic Dominance in "opaque sweetening" cases is made by Hare (2010, 240).

A sequential choice situation that leads an agent, choosing on the basis of her preferences, to make a sequence of choices that is unambiguously worse than an available alternative is called a *money pump*.[34] Here is an example of the sort of money pump to which fanatics are vulnerable:[35]

**Don't Let the Green Grass Fool You** A fair blue coin will be flipped until it lands tails. You are offered, initially, a choice between two prospects based on these coin flips. The possible outcomes of these prospects come from a sequence $o_1$, $o_2$, etc where, as above, $\langle o_{n+1}, 2^{-(n+1)}, o^- \rangle$ is always strictly preferred to $\langle o_n \rangle$, for some baseline outcome $o^-$ strictly worse than $o_1$. The prospect Blue$^+$ will give you outcome $o_2$ if the blue coin lands tails on the first flip, $o_3$ if it lands tails on the second flip, etc. The prospect Blue$^{++}$ will give you $o_3$ if the blue coin lands tails on the first flip, $o_4$ if it lands tails on the second flip, etc. Thus, for each possible outcome of the blue coin tosses, Blue$^{++}$ will give you a strictly better outcome than Blue$^+$.

But there's a catch: If you choose Blue$^{++}$, then after seeing the flips of the blue coin, you will be offered the chance to switch to a different prospect. This alternative prospect is based on the flips of a *green* coin, also fair and uncorrelated with the blue coin. The prospect Green will give you $o_1$ if the green coin lands tails on the first flip, $o_2$ if it lands tails on the second flip, etc.

This sequence of choices is illustrated in Figure 2. (In this diagram, squares represent choices, circles represent chance events, and numbers on the lines connecting two nodes represent probabilities.)

How should you act in this situation, given your fanatical preferences? Intuitively, you should reason as follows: You know that you prefer Green to each of its possible outcomes, and therefore to each of the possible outcomes of Blue$^+$ and Blue$^{++}$. If you choose Blue$^{++}$, therefore, after learning its outcome – whatever that outcome turns out to be – you will prefer to switch to Green. Thus your initial choice (at node 0) is really not between Blue$^+$ and Blue$^{++}$, but between Blue$^+$ and Green. And you should prefer Blue$^+$ to Green, since it gives you the prospect $\langle (o_2, \frac{1}{2}), (o_3, \frac{1}{4}), (o_4, \frac{1}{8}), \ldots \rangle$ instead of $\langle (o_1, \frac{1}{2}), (o_2, \frac{1}{4}), (o_3, \frac{1}{8}), \ldots \rangle$ (and $o^{n+1}$ is in every case strictly better than $o_n$). So you should choose Blue$^+$.

---

[34] Sometimes money pumps are characterized more narrowly, as involving *exploitation* or requiring that the agent "pay for something that she could have kept for free." But I ignore these features, which I see as noncentral, in the following discussion. For a useful recent introduction to money-pump arguments, see Gustafsson (2022).

[35] This example is a modification of one described in Russell and Isaacs (2021, 181n). A closely related dynamic inconsistency argument, directed against unbounded utilities in the context of expected utility theory, can be found in Hammond (1998).

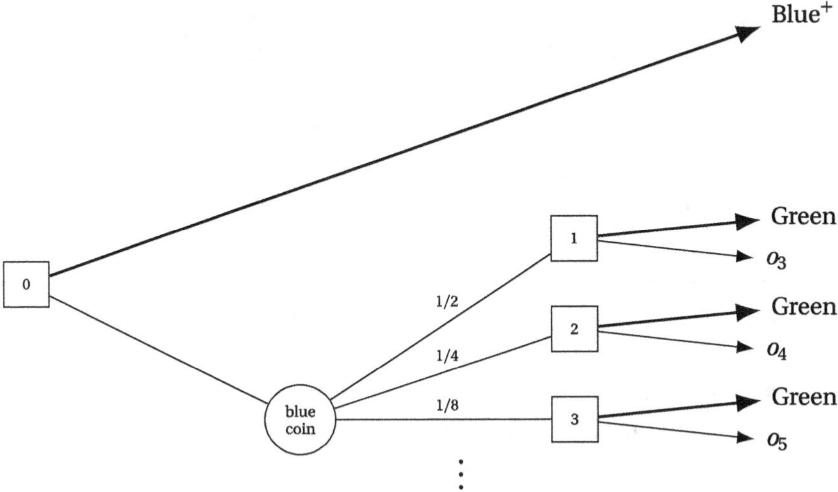


**Figure 2** A money pump for fanatics

But this means that, with certainty, you will end up with a worse outcome than you could have had by choosing Blue$^{++}$ and declining the option to switch to Green. And that seems bad.

To turn this into a more formal argument against fanaticism, we need three principles of rationality for sequential choice:

**Preferential Choice** When an agent faces a terminal choice (one not followed by any further choice nodes), she is rationally required to choose an act whose prospect is maximally preferred. That is, she is rationally prohibited from choosing an act if there is another act whose prospect she strictly prefers.

**Sophisticated Choice** When an agent faces a choice where, conditional on any act she might choose, she can predict with certainty what choice she will make at any subsequent choice nodes, then she is rationally required to treat those predictable future choices as fixed and to choose an act that leads to a maximally preferred prospect given those choices.

**Non-Domination** If an agent has rational preferences, chooses rationally based on those preferences, knows the structure of the sequential choice situation she faces, and is certain that at future nodes she'll choose rationally, update her beliefs rationally, and not change her preferences, then she will not take any action that is *dominated* in the sense that any pure strategy that takes that action is stochastically dominated by a strategy that does not.

In the preceding example, Stochastic Dominance and Transitivity imply that you strictly prefer the prospect Green to every possible outcome of Blue$^{++}$

(as we saw in Section 4.1). Preferential Choice therefore implies that you will be rationally required to choose Green at each of nodes 1, 2, 3, etc. Sophisticated Choice then implies that, if you know the structure of the choice situation and are certain of your own future rationality, you should choose Blue$^+$ at node 0 if and only if you prefer Blue$^+$ to Green. Stochastic Dominance implies that you *do* prefer Blue$^+$ to Green. Therefore, if you choose rationally based on your preferences, you'll go up at node 0. Any pure strategy that goes up at node 0 yields the prospect Blue$^+$. But there's an available strategy that yields the stochastically dominant prospect Blue$^{++}$ – namely, going down at every choice node, that is, choosing Blue$^{++}$ and sticking with it. (Indeed, Blue$^{++}$ *statewise* dominates Blue$^+$, since it yields a better outcome regardless of the outcome of the blue coin flips.) Thus, by Non-Domination, your preferences must be irrational.

Although this example relied on Narrow Positive Fanaticism, we could give an exactly parallel argument for Narrow Negative Fanaticism, using a "negative" St. Petersburg prospect with an infinite sequence of increasingly bad outcomes. We can therefore conclude the following:

> Given Full Domain (and a domain of sequential choice situations large enough to include cases like the anti-fanatical money pump in Figure 2), the principles of Stochastic Dominance, Transitivity, Preferential Choice, Sophisticated Choice, and Non-Domination rule out Narrow Positive Fanaticism and Narrow Negative Fanaticism. Indeed, these principles imply that preferences satisfying either Narrow Positive Fanaticism or Narrow Negative Fanaticism are rationally prohibited.[36]

I see this as quite a strong argument against fanaticism. Stochastic Dominance and Transitivity are very plausible and widely accepted, and the uses to which those principles were put in the preceding argument are more clear-cut than some of the edge cases in which they have been challenged. Sophisticated Choice strikes me as clearly correct, and in any case, it's not obvious that giving it up would help the fanatic avoid money pumps.[37] One option for the fanatic is to give up Preferential Choice in favor of "resolute choice," which holds roughly that at the start of a sequential choice situation, you should adopt a strategy that yields a maximally preferred prospect from your present perspective,

---

[36] I don't treat this as a formal result only because we have not made the framework of sequential choice situations or the principles of sequential rationality fully precise. But this can be easily done.

[37] The major alternative to Sophisticated Choice, typically called "naive choice," tells an agent to simply follow whatever strategy looks best from her current perspective, even if she can predict that she will deviate from that strategy at later choice nodes. But a fanatic who follows naive choice is still vulnerable to money pumps – for an example, see Russell and Isaacs (2021, 182).

then choose according to that strategy even if it contradicts your later preferences. This is a very general strategy for avoiding money pumps. But it relies on attributing a dubious normative authority to past decisions. It's easy to see why you should follow through on your plans when the temptation to deviate from them stems from weakness of will or other forms of irrationality, but much harder to see why the preferences of your past self should override the *rationally formed* preferences of your present self in determining what it's rational for you to do right now.[38]

The best option for the fanatic, I think, is to deny Non-Domination. It certainly seems strange that rationality should require an agent to make dominated choices. One thing we would like norms of practical rationality to do is to make us *effective* at pursuing desirable outcomes; forcing us to settle for prospects that are unambiguously worse than available alternatives seems antithetical to that. But perhaps in infinitary contexts, absolute invulnerability to this sort of failure is simply too much to ask of rationality (Arntzenius et al., 2004). If a combination of basic moral and decision-theoretic principles (like Anteriority, Positive/Negative Additions, Superdominance, and Transitivity) require us to have certain preferences, then we must follow those preferences where they lead. And the fact that we cannot reliably coordinate our choices at different times and different branches of the decision tree to secure the prospect we might ideally like (e.g., cannot commit ourselves to going down at nodes 1, 2, 3, etc, thereby securing the prospect $Blue^{++}$) should be regarded as an unfortunate feature of our situation, not proof of irrationality. If I were convinced of principles that entailed fanaticism, then I would at least be open to biting the bullet in this way. Nevertheless, vulnerability to money pumps is clearly an unwelcome conclusion, and puts significant weight on the scales against fanaticism.

## 5 The Case for Anti-Fanaticism

We have just seen an argument against fanaticism. Is this also an argument *for* the diametrically opposing thesis of *anti*-fanaticism? More specifically, is it an argument for the thesis of Narrow Anti-Fanaticism that we introduced in Section 2.3? Not quite. In this very brief section, I'll describe what is needed to bridge the gap.

Narrow Fanaticism asserts that we should be willing to pay an arbitrarily high price for an arbitrarily small chance of an astronomically good outcome, if it's

---

[38] For recent discussions of resolute choice, see Andreou (2022, §3) and Gustafsson (2022, §7). In the main text, I assume what Gustafsson calls the "counter-preferential" understanding of resolute choice. Several other versions of resoluteness are possible, as he describes, though not all of them would serve the fanatic's purposes in the present context.

good enough, or to avoid an arbitrarily small chance of an astronomically bad outcome, if it's bad enough. Narrow Anti-Fanaticism asserts that there is some price high enough, and some probability small enough, that we should *refuse* to pay that price to gain or avoid that probability of any outcome, no matter how astronomically good or bad. One way that both theses could be false is if we are rationally permitted to have either sort of preference. But the argument in the last section purported to show that preferences satisfying Narrow Fanaticism are not just nonmandatory but positively irrational.

Another way that both Narrow Fanaticism and Narrow Anti-Fanaticism could be false is if it is rationally permissible, or even rationally required, to have *incomplete* preferences with respect to extreme tradeoffs, that render one's preferences neither fanatical nor anti-fanatical. The key premise needed to turn an argument for the irrationality of Narrow Fanaticism into an argument for Narrow Anti-Fanaticism is to rule out such gappy preferences. Though we could try to accomplish this in more targeted ways, let's focus on the general principle that an agent must always have a preference between any two prospects.

**Completeness**  It is rationally required that, for any prospects $P_i$ and $P_j$, either $P_i$ is weakly preferred to $P_j$, or $P_j$ is weakly preferred to $P_i$, or both. (Equivalently, either one prospect is strictly preferred to the other or they are preferred equally.)

This principle, with a couple auxiliary assumptions, gets us from the arguments of the last section to Narrow Anti-Fanaticism.

**Proposition 3** *Given Completeness, Transitivity, and Stochastic Dominance, the rational impermissibility of preferences that satisfy Narrow Positive Fanaticism implies Narrow Positive Anti-Fanaticism; and likewise, the rational impermissibility of preferences that satisfy Narrow Negative Fanaticism implies Narrow Negative Anti-Fanaticism.*

*Proof* As usual, we focus on the positive case. The impermissibility of preferences that satisfy Narrow Positive Fanaticism means it's rationally required that for some outcomes $o^+ >_0 o^-$ and probability $p > 0$, there is no outcome $o^{*+}$ such that $\langle o^{*+}, p', o^- \rangle > \langle o^+ \rangle$ for all $p' \geq p$. Now, let $p''$ be a probability that is strictly less than $p$ but greater than 0. Our aim is to show that, for any $o^{*+}$, $\langle o^+ \rangle > \langle o^{*+}, p''', o^- \rangle$ for all $p''' \leq p''$. If $o^+ \succsim_0 o^{*+}$, this follows directly from Stochastic Dominance. So we can focus on the case where $o^{*+} >_0 o^+$. The impermissibility of preferences satisfying Narrow Positive Fanaticism means there must be some $p' \geq p$ such that $\langle o^{*+}, p', o^- \rangle \not> \langle o^+ \rangle$. Completeness then implies that $\langle o^+ \rangle \succsim \langle o^{*+}, p', o^- \rangle$. Stochastic Dominance entails that $\langle o^{*+}, p', o^- \rangle > \langle o^{*+}, p''', o^- \rangle$ for any $p''' < p'$, which includes any $p''' \leq p''$. It follows from Transitivity that $\langle o^+ \rangle > \langle o^{*+}, p''', o^- \rangle$ for all $p''' \leq p''$. $\qquad\square$

Transitivity and Stochastic Dominance are both very plausible, and as in the last section, the uses to which we have put these principles here are not especially controversial. The question of whether arguments for the irrationality of Narrow Fanaticism are also arguments for Narrow Anti-Fanaticism, therefore, turns on whether we should accept Completeness. We will table this question for now, and return to it in Section 7.

## 6 The Case against Anti-Fanaticism

The preceding discussion has been largely unfavorable to fanaticism. In this section, however, it will be anti-fanaticism's turn in the hot seat. But the case I will make against anti-fanaticism is different in kind to the case against fanaticism. Specifically, I will not argue that Narrow Anti-Fanaticism, the version of anti-fanaticism that we have had in mind thus far, violates any principles of rationality. Instead I will argue that Narrow Anti-Fanaticism neither does justice to our intuitive resistance to fanaticism nor – more importantly – rules out fanatical applications of expected value reasoning in important real-world contexts of high-stakes decision-making. Insofar as we want to do justice to our intuitions, and to avoid giving extreme weight to tiny effects on the probability of extreme outcomes in our real-world choices, we must adopt a more general form of anti-fanaticism. And that more general thesis *does* violate important principles of rationality. After setting out this argument, I'll consider its implications for the two canonical decision-theoretic recipes for avoiding fanaticism: bounded utility and small-probability discounting.[39]

## 6.1 Small Probabilities and Small Differences in Probability

Narrow Fanaticism and Narrow Anti-Fanaticism are attractively simple theses. But they don't fully capture the question of whether we should give potentially unlimited weight to arbitrarily small probabilities. That's because they only consider a special case, where an agent is choosing between certainty on the one hand and a binary prospect involving a tiny probability of an astronomically good/bad outcome on the other. The more general (and more realistic) case is a choice between two prospects that *differ* slightly in how they distribute probability between much better and much worse outcomes – in other words, a case where the agent must decide how much she is willing to pay in order

---

[39] This section is adapted from Tarsney (2025a).

**Table 3** Left: A simple choice between certainty of a small gain and a small probability of a large gain. Right: A small probability difference without a small probability. The choice is between a sure gain of 1 and a small ($2\varepsilon$) increase in the probability of a large gain $\left(\frac{1}{\varepsilon}\right)$.

| (A) SMALL PROBABILITY | | |
|---|---|---|
| | $s_1\ (1-2\varepsilon)$ | $s_2\ (2\varepsilon)$ |
| $P_1$ | 1 | 1 |
| $P_2$ | 0 | $\frac{1}{\varepsilon}$ |

| (B) SMALL PROBABILITY DIFFERENCE | | |
|---|---|---|
| | $s_1\ (0.5-\varepsilon)$ | $s_2\ (0.5+\varepsilon)$ |
| $P_3$ | $\frac{1}{\varepsilon}+1$ | 1 |
| $P_4$ | 0 | $\frac{1}{\varepsilon}$ |

to *shift* a small amount of probability from a much worse outcome to a much better outcome.

To see the difference, consider the two choice situations described in Tables 3a and 3b, each of which involves a choice between two prospects, with uncertainty between two possible states of nature. The first is a simple choice between certainty of a small gain (1) and a small probability ($2\varepsilon$) of a large gain ($\frac{1}{\varepsilon}$). The second case is slightly more complicated: Here the astronomically large gain $\frac{1}{\varepsilon}$ has a "baseline" probability of $0.5 - \varepsilon$, and the choice is between taking a sure gain (improving each outcome by 1) or slightly *increasing* that baseline probability (by $2\varepsilon$) – in this case, by moving the astronomically good outcome from a less probable to a more probable state. In the second case, small probabilities are nowhere to be seen – every state, and every outcome, has a quite substantial probability. What is small is the *difference* in probability between $s_1$ and $s_2$, and hence between the probabilities of a very good outcome associated with $P_3$ and $P_4$ respectively. It seems to me, though, that anyone who finds expected value maximization counterintuitively fanatical in the first case will have the same intuition about the second case.

Choices like 3b are also much more common and realistic than choices like 3a. Consider, for instance, two important real-world cases: voting and existential risk mitigation. If you are deciding whether it is worth your while to vote in an election, in terms of the difference you might make to the outcome, it's never the case that your preferred candidate is certain to lose if you don't vote, but has a tiny probability of winning if you do; nor that they are certain to win if you vote, but have a tiny probability of losing if you don't. Rather, they have some intermediate probability of winning, which your vote would slightly increase. Similarly, if you are deciding whether to devote some unit of resources to mitigating existential risks (from engineered pandemics, nuclear war, AI or the like) or to providing some more certain good (like direct cash transfers to the poor), the situation is not that near-term human extinction is certain if you do not act to prevent it, and your intervention represents humanity's only slim hope of survival; nor that humanity is certain to survive if you act to assure its survival, and the only chance of doom comes from your inaction. Rather, there is some nontrivial probability that humanity will succumb to a near-term existential catastrophe, and some nontrivial probability that it will not, and your intervention (if well-chosen) might very slightly reduce the former probability and increase the latter.

Insofar as we find fanaticism counterintuitive, its counterintuitiveness is not confined to simple choices between risk and certainty, but extends to the more general case of small changes to an uncertain baseline prospect. And insofar as anti-fanaticism is meant to resist fanatical applications of expected value reasoning in real-world contexts, it must apply to this more general case as well. The thesis must be that it is irrational to trade certainty of a substantial gain for arbitrarily small shifts in probability from one outcome to another.

## 6.2 Anti-Fanaticism Generalized

Our next task, then, is to make that informal thesis precise. To do this, we need to introduce two new concepts. In the simple context of small probabilities, the "safe" option could be characterized as yielding a single outcome with certainty. In the more general context, we assume that astronomically better and astronomically worse outcomes will have some non-zero probability whatever option one chooses, and so the safe option can no longer be characterized in that way. We can characterize it instead, however, as offering a sure *improvement* to the outcome of the baseline prospect. To illustrate: In the case of voting, if you choose not to vote, you can instead spend an hour watching television. This doesn't deliver a single outcome with certainty since (among other things) it leaves you uncertain who will win the election – but it does mean that both possible election outcomes will be *improved*, from your perspective, by the addition of one hour of television. Similarly, if instead of spending a fixed sum of money to mitigate existential risks, you spend it on direct cash transfers to the very poor, you are not left with certainty of any particular outcome, but instead with certainty that whatever otherwise would have happened will be improved by certain very poor people being made slightly less poor.[40]

---

[40] Of course, in reality even these improvements are not literally *certain*. But treating them that way is, as far as I can see, a harmless idealization for present purposes that does not sacrifice any interesting generality.

We therefore introduce the following two concepts:

An *improvement* is a function $I : \mathbb{O} \to \mathbb{O}$ that maps every outcome to a strictly better outcome if one exists, or else to an equally good outcome.

A *worsening* is a function $W : \mathbb{O} \to \mathbb{O}$ that maps every outcome to a strictly worse outcome if one exists, or else to an equally good outcome.

Paradigmatically, an improvement might be a fixed change that can be applied to any outcome, like giving one individual an additional year of life at a fixed level of positive well-being. But the concept is more flexible than that, and does not presuppose that there is any concrete change that can be applied to every possible outcome and that always makes an outcome (even weakly) better. An improvement (or worsening) *could* correspond to intuitively very different concrete changes to different outcomes.

In rough terms, the generalized form of anti-fanaticism will say (in the positive case) that a large enough *improvement* to every outcome in a baseline prospect should always be preferred to a small enough shift in probability from one outcome to another, no matter how disparate those outcomes might be. But this gloss requires an important caveat: One extreme way of being an anti-fanatic is to hold that some outcomes and prospects are "good enough," in the sense that a rational agent may be completely indifferent to any further improvements. Formally, let's say that a prospect $P$ is *maximal* if no other prospect is strictly preferred to it, and that an outcome $o$ is maximal if the prospect $\langle o \rangle$ is maximal. (Likewise, $P$ is *minimal* if no other prospect is strictly *dis*preferred to it, and $o$ is minimal if $\langle o \rangle$ is minimal.) In a choice between a sure improvement and a small probability shift, the prospect resulting from the small shift might be maximal, either because the baseline prospect itself consisted entirely of maximal outcomes or because it involved only a small probability of a nonmaximal outcome, which the small probability shift eliminates. In this case, the anti-fanatic need not require that the sure improvement be strictly preferred.

These points in hand, we can now state a more general version of anti-fanaticism:

**General Positive Anti-Fanaticism**  It is rationally required that there is some improvement $I$ and probability $p > 0$ such that, for any outcomes $o^{*+} >_O o^-$ and any probability $q < 1$, the prospect $\langle I(o^{*+}), q, I(o^-) \rangle$ is weakly preferred to $\langle o^{*+}, q + p', o^- \rangle$ for any $p' \leq p$ (and $\leq 1 - q$). Moreover, this preference is strict unless $o^{*+}$ and $o^-$ are both maximal, or $o^{*+}$ is maximal and $q + p' = 1$.

**General Negative Anti-Fanaticism**  It is rationally required that there is some worsening $W$ and probability $p > 0$ such that, for any outcomes $o^+ >_O o^{*-}$

and any probability $q < 1$, the prospect $\langle o^{*-}, q+p', o^+ \rangle$ is weakly preferred to $\langle W(o^{*-}), q, W(o^+) \rangle$ for any $p' \leq p$ (and $\leq 1 - q$). Moreover, this preference is strict unless $o^+$ and $o^{*-}$ are both minimal, or $o^{*-}$ is minimal and $q + p' = 1$.

Intuitively, General Positive Anti-Fanaticism says that there is some improvement $I$ large enough, and (non-zero) probability $p$ small enough, that given a choice between (i) improving every outcome in your "baseline" prospect by $I$ or (ii) increasing the probability of an astronomically good outcome by $p$, you always at least weakly prefer the former. For example, perhaps you should always prefer adding twenty happy years to someone's life over increasing the probability of any outcome (no matter how good) by $10^{-30}$ or less. And General Negative Anti-Fanaticism says that there is some worsening $W$ large enough, and (non-zero) probability $p$ small enough, that given a choice between (i) worsening every outcome in your baseline prospect by $W$ or (ii) increasing the probability of an astronomically bad outcome by $p$, you always at least weakly prefer the latter. For instance, perhaps you should always be willing to increase the risk of any outcome (no matter how bad) by $10^{-30}$ or less rather than *shorten* a happy life by twenty years. *General Anti-Fanaticism* is the conjunction of these two theses.

General Anti-Fanaticism is stronger than Narrow Anti-Fanaticism, since it universally quantifies over the baseline probability $q$, where Narrow Anti-Fanaticism only covers the special case of $q = 0$.[41]

## 6.3 The Argument from Acyclicity

Anyone who wants to do justice to our anti-fanatical intuitions and to resist fanatical real-world applications of expected value reasoning must, I have argued, endorse not just Narrow but General Anti-Fanaticism. But unfortunately, this thesis is subject to a very powerful objection. To state the objection, we need to introduce a few new principles.

**No Best Outcome** For every outcome, there is a strictly better outcome.

**No Worst Outcome** For every outcome, there is a strictly worse outcome.

**Minimal Dominance** If $o_i >_O o_j$, then it is rationally required that $\langle o_i \rangle > \langle o_j \rangle$.

**Acyclicity** It is rationally required that, if $P_1 > P_2, P_2 > P_3, \ldots, P_{n-1} > P_n$, then it's not the case that $P_n > P_1$.

---

[41] More precisely, General Positive Anti-Fanaticism implies Narrow Positive Anti-Fanaticism given the minimal assumption that there are two outcomes $o^{*+} >_O o^-$ where $o^-$ is nonmaximal (and an analogous assumption is needed in the negative case). For the derivation, see Tarsney (2025a, fn. 7).

These principles are very weak, and hard to deny. No Best Outcome and No Worst Outcome do not imply anything like unboundedness of cardinal value or utility. They only assert that there is always *some* way of making an outcome at least a little better/worse – for instance, by extending a happy/unhappy life, or adding a positive/negative experience to a life without changing its duration. Minimal Dominance is perhaps the weakest possible expression of the idea that the desirability of a prospect depends on the value of its possible outcomes. It's much weaker than Stochastic Dominance, and even weaker than Superdominance.[42] Finally, Acyclicity is the least controversial of the standard coherence constraints on rational preference associated with expected utility theory. It is implied by, but significantly weaker than, Transitivity. And it is supported by a particularly compelling and straightforward money-pump argument (Gustafsson, 2022, Ch. 2).

But surprisingly, General Anti-Fanaticism is incompatible with these very weak principles. Specifically:

**Proposition 4** *Acyclicity, Minimal Dominance, and No Best Outcome rule out General Positive Anti-Fanaticism. Acyclicity, Minimal Dominance, and No Worst Outcome rule out General Negative Anti-Fanaticism.*

*Proof* As usual, we'll focus on the positive case (the negative case being exactly parallel). No Best Outcome and Minimal Dominance together imply that no outcome is maximal. (For every outcome $o$ there's a strictly better outcome $o'$, and $\langle o' \rangle$ must be strictly preferred to $\langle o \rangle$.) General Positive Anti-Fanaticism therefore requires without qualification that there is some improvement $I$ and positive probability $p$ such that, for any outcomes $o^{*+} \succsim o$ $o^{-}$ and probability $q < 1$, the prospect $\langle I(o^{*+}), q, I(o^{-}) \rangle$ is strictly preferred to $\langle o^{*+}, q + p', o^{-} \rangle$ for any $p' \leq p$ and $\leq 1 - q$.[43] Given such an $I$ and $p$, choose an integer $n$ such that $\frac{1}{n} \leq p$, and an arbitrary "baseline" outcome $o$. Then consider the prospects shown in Table 4. Here we have $n$ equiprobable states and $n + 1$ prospects. The various possible outcomes are generated from the baseline outcome $o$ by applying improvement $I$ one or more times, with $I^k$ representing $k$ iterations of $I$ (i.e., the result of applying $I$ to $o$, $k$ times over). At each step

---

[42] Although I'm not aware of anyone who explicitly rejects Superdominance, we saw in Section 3.4 that there is a potential reason to reject it in infinitary contexts, if one is sufficiently committed to individualist principles like Anteriority. But as far as I can tell, no similar tension exists between Anteriority and Minimal Dominance, in which case even this potential reason for skepticism is unavailable.

[43] No Best Outcome and Minimal Dominance aren't used in the rest of the proof. This means that a stronger version of General Anti-Fanaticism requiring the sure improvement to be strictly preferred in every case would be intrinsically cyclic.

**Table 4** An illustration of the cyclicity objection to General
Anti-Fanaticism

|  | $s_1 \left(\frac{1}{n}\right)$ | $s_2 \left(\frac{1}{n}\right)$ | $s_3 \left(\frac{1}{n}\right)$ | $\cdots$ | $s_n \left(\frac{1}{n}\right)$ |
|---|---|---|---|---|---|
| $P_0$ | $I^n(o)$ | $I^n(o)$ | $I^n(o)$ | $\cdots$ | $I^n(o)$ |
| $P_1$ | $I(o)$ | $I^{n+1}(o)$ | $I^{n+1}(o)$ | $\cdots$ | $I^{n+1}(o)$ |
| $P_2$ | $I^2(o)$ | $I^2(o)$ | $I^{n+2}(o)$ | $\cdots$ | $I^{n+2}(o)$ |
| $\vdots$ | $\vdots$ | $\vdots$ | $\vdots$ | $\ddots$ | $\vdots$ |
| $P_n$ | $I^n(o)$ | $I^n(o)$ | $I^n(o)$ | $\cdots$ | $I^n(o)$ |

from $P_{i-1}$ to $P_i$, we make two changes: We "slightly" improve the outcome in every state by adding one iteration of $I$, while "astronomically" *worsening* the outcome in state $s_i$ by *removing* $n$ iterations of $I$. (Here "slightly" and "astronomically" do not imply anything about cardinal value – they just mean "by a single iteration of $I$" and "by many iterations of $I$" respectively.)

General Positive Anti-Fanaticism implies that each step from $P_{i-1}$ to $P_i$ is a strict improvement: In a choice between improving every outcome by $I$ or shifting probability $\frac{1}{n} \leq p$ to an astronomically better outcome, we always prefer the former. Thus, $P_1 > P_0$, $P_2 > P_1$, and so on. But at the end of this sequence of strict improvements, we end up exactly where we started – $P_n$ is identical to $P_0$! So we have a cycle: $P_n > P_{n-1} > \ldots P_1 > P_n$. $\qquad \square$

This result constitutes an argument against General Anti-Fanaticism, which I will call the *Argument from Acyclicity*. This argument strikes me as quite compelling. In particular, it relies on much weaker premises than extant arguments for fanaticism, like the Spectrum Argument, the Argument from Anteriority, and other arguments discussed in the recent literature (e.g., by Wilkinson, 2022; Russell, 2023; Beckstead and Thomas, 2024), which rely on substantial ethical assumptions like Prospect Separability (fn. 28), or substantive constraints on agents' risk attitudes. No Best/Worst Outcome and Minimal Dominance strike me as almost undeniable. The easiest principle for the anti-fanatic to give up, I think, is Acyclicity. The cost of this move is somewhat mitigated by the fact that the cycles into which General Anti-Fanaticism leads us may be *extremely* long. For instance, an agent who ignores probability differences smaller than $10^{-15}$ need not have any preference cycles shorter than $10^{15}$ steps. (This will, among other things, make her fairly difficult to money pump – it will require a setup in which she faces, or believes herself to face, a potential sequence of choices at least $10^{15}$ nodes long.) Still, we should not let the juxtaposition with other, even-less-deniable principles fool us: Acyclicity is an extremely plausible principle, and denying it is a very serious cost. I conclude, therefore, that we should reject General Anti-Fanaticism.[44]

## 6.4 Bounded MEU

Let's now consider what the preceding argument tells us about two views in normative decision theory that have been treated as paradigmatic forms of anti-fanaticism: bounded expected utility maximization (Bounded MEU) and small-probability discounting.

Beginning with the former: Bounded MEU combines MEU (as stated in Section 2.5) with the claim that utilities should be bounded: There should be some real numbers $\bar{u}$ and $\underline{u}$ such that no outcome receives a utility greater than $\bar{u}$ or less than $\underline{u}$. This need not imply that there is a highest-utility or a lowest-utility outcome, since the utilities of outcomes may approach the bounds without ever reaching them. It does, however, satisfy Narrow Anti-Fanaticism: For instance, given a choice between certainty of an outcome with near-maximal utility and a risky prospect that is almost certain to yield a significantly worse outcome, any long-shot reward will be at most slightly better than the sure thing, and so insufficient to justify the risk.

Bounded MEU is perhaps the most orthodox form of orthodox decision theory. The requirement of boundedness is commonly motivated by the need to avoid St. Petersburg-like prospects (see fn. 30), whose paradoxical features are not just counterintuitive but also in tension with central features of expected utility theory.[45] But in addition to these more technical arguments, some expected utility theorists have seen the avoidance of counterintuitive fanaticism as a sufficient justification for boundedness.[46]

---

[44] In Section 5, we saw that an argument against Narrow Fanaticism could be transformed into an argument for Narrow Anti-Fanaticism, with the additional assumption of Completeness. Can we do something similar here, transforming the Argument from Acyclicity against General Anti-Fanaticism into an argument for fanaticism? Sort of, but not really. Assuming Completeness, and strengthening Acyclicity to Transitivity, does allow us to construct an argument for a form of fanaticism, but only a very weak form – so weak, in fact, that it's compatible with Narrow Anti-Fanaticism! For details, see §8 of Tarsney (2025a).

[45] In particular, such prospects violate both Continuity and an infinitary generalization of Independence, the essential characteristic principle of expected utility theory. On the other hand, Goodsell (2024) shows that it's possible to construct a consistent decision theory that allows unbounded utility and prospects without finite expectations, while still satisfying many of the core principles of expected utility.

[46] For instance, Aumann writes: "Unbounded utility would lead to counterintuitive conclusions even without the St. Petersburg paradox. If Paul's utility were unbounded, then for any fixed prospect x (e.g., a long, happy, and useful life), there would be a prospect y with the property that Paul would prefer a lottery yielding y with probability $\frac{1}{10^{100}}$ and death with the complementary probability to the prospect x. This, I think, is about as hard to swallow as the idea of infinite utility" (Aumann, 1977, 444). Machina (1982, 283–284) expresses similar sentiments.

On the other hand, Bounded MEU itself has some fairly counterintuitive features. It requires extreme risk-aversion with respect to outcomes near the upper bound of the utility function, and extreme risk-seeking for outcomes near the lower bound. (For discussion of this point, see §3.3 of Beckstead and Thomas (2024).) And, in the moral context, the combination of Bounded MEU with many plausible outcome axiologies will result in violations of individualist principles like Anteriority.[47]

But my main purpose here isn't to argue against Bounded MEU. (In particular, as discussed in Section 3.5, I don't think that conflict with Anteriority is a decisive objection.) Rather, the upshot of the preceding discussion is that despite appearances (and despite satisfying Narrow Anti-Fanaticism), Bounded MEU in its standard form is not generally anti-fanatical: Since Bounded MEU is acyclic, Proposition 4 implies that, given No Best Outcome, No Worst Outcome, and Minimal Dominance, it will not satisfy General Anti-Fanaticism.

The intuitive explanation for this fact (focusing, as usual, on the positive case) is that as we approach the upper bound of the utility function, the marginal utility of any given improvement must decrease very rapidly. Consider, for instance, a choice between shifting a small amount of probability from a mediocre outcome (near the middle of the utility function) to an astronomically good outcome (near the upper bound), or else applying some fixed improvement to every outcome. If the baseline probability of the astronomically good outcome is already high, then the increment to *expected* utility from the latter option will be very small, since the improvement is most likely to be applied to an outcome that already has nearly maximal utility.

As a concrete illustration, consider a choice between slightly reducing the risk of premature human extinction and creating some fixed benefit, for example, saving a life. Suppose you think that the baseline risk of premature extinction is fairly low, and that if we avoid it, we are very likely to achieve a very good future. Then, as a bounded expected utility maximizer, you will be likely to prefer even a tiny reduction in the already-small risk of human extinction to a sure improvement that is very likely to improve an already-very-good world, and so counts for very little.

It's *possible* for a bounded expected utility maximizer to satisfy General Anti-Fanaticism, by assigning some outcome(s) maximal utility and some

---

[47] Specifically, it follows from Proposition 1 that Bounded MEU will violate Anteriority when combined with any axiology that satisfies either Positive or Negative Additions, given Minimal Dominance. (Bounded MEU necessarily satisfies Transitivity and does not satisfy Narrow Positive or Negative Fanaticism. Given Minimal Dominance, it will also satisfy Superdominance.) Kosonen (2022, Ch. 1) shows in particular that the combination of Bounded MEU with a total utilitarian axiology violates a principle closely related to Anteriority.

outcome(s) minimal utility. (We might call this *Compact* MEU, since it requires the range of the utility function to be not just bounded but compact.) General Anti-Fanaticism is then satisfied because (focusing on the positive case) we can find an improvement that maps every outcome to an outcome with maximal utility. Applying this improvement to every outcome in a baseline prospect yields a prospect with maximal expected utility, which is weakly preferred to any long-shot alternative, and strictly preferred unless that alternative consists entirely of maximal outcomes. Unlike the standard form of Bounded MEU, however, this view must give up either No Best/Worst Outcome or Minimal Dominance. I won't say more about Compact MEU, for the sake of space and because it strikes me as quite implausible. (I say a bit more in Tarsney (2025a, §6).) But it shows that it's possible, in principle, to satisfy General Anti-Fanaticism within the confines of expected utility theory, without preference cycles.

## 6.5 Small-Probability Discounting

The other commonly proposed strategy for avoiding both fanaticism and the paradoxical implications of St. Petersburg-like prospects is to simply *ignore* small probabilities. This idea has a long history, going back at least to a 1714 letter from Nicolaus Bernoulli to Pierre Rémond de Montmort. And it has recently experienced something of a revival, being advocated by Smith (2014) and Monton (2019), and seriously entertained by Buchak (2013, 73–74) and Hong (2024).[48]

Small-probability discounting can take many forms. The simplest forms are *state discounting*, which ignores very improbable states, and *outcome discounting*, which ignores very improbable outcomes. The *very* simplest versions of these approaches, which tell us to ignore all states or outcomes with probabilities below some fixed threshold $t$, seem unworkable, since there will be situations where *all* states and outcomes have probabilities below that threshold (Arrow, 1951, 414–415). But more sophisticated versions of state/outcome discounting avoid this problem, for example, by ignoring all states/outcomes that are at least $n$ times less probable than the *most* probable state/outcome, or ignoring the *least* probable states/outcomes up to a total probability of $t$. Even with these amendments, though, state and outcome discounting are subject to powerful objections. They are implausibly sensitive to small differences that can turn a single high-probability state/outcome into many low-probability states/outcomes (Beckstead and Thomas, 2024, §2.3). And they can easily

---

[48] For a detailed history of the idea of small-probability discounting, see Monton (2019).

run afoul of dominance principles (Isaacs, 2016; Kosonen, 2022, 151–164; Beckstead and Thomas, 2024, §2.3).

A more promising way of ignoring small probabilities is *tail discounting*.[49] Roughly, tail discounting tells us to ignore the very-worst-case and very-best-case outcomes of every prospect, up to a certain probability (say, 0.01%) – either simply removing those worst-case and best-case outcomes from each prospect altogether (and renormalizing the remaining probabilities), or rounding those outcomes up/down (so that, for instance, any possible outcomes better than the 99.99th percentile of possible outcomes are "rounded down" to the 99.99th percentile outcome, and any possible outcomes worse than the 0.01st percentile are "rounded up" to the 0.01st percentile outcome). We can then apply expected value maximization, or another decision rule, to these "truncated" prospects.

Tail discounting has significant advantages over state and outcome discounting. In particular, its verdicts don't depend on how we individuate states or outcomes, and it therefore avoids extreme sensitivity to small differences between outcomes. Moreover, it can be straightforwardly reconciled with Stochastic Dominance and other dominance principles, by stipulating that the truncated portions of a prospect are used as tiebreakers (Beckstead and Thomas, 2024, §2.3).

On the other hand, tail discounting is still subject to significant objections. Since it violates the Independence axiom of expected utility theory, it's susceptible to money pumps (Kosonen, 2022, 178–189; Kosonen, 2024). And in the moral context, as with Bounded MEU, it's prone to conflict with principles like Anteriority. (For instance, since tail-discounted MEV satisfies Transitivity and Superdominance but not Narrow Fanaticism, Proposition 1 implies that it will violate Anteriority given any outcome axiology that satisfies either Positive or Negative Additions.)

But as with Bounded MEU, my main purpose here isn't to adjudicate the arguments for and against tail discounting. Rather, once again, the upshot of the arguments from Sections 6.1–6.3 is that whatever its other merits and despite initial appearances, tail discounting does not fully vindicate our anti-fanatical intuitions. This is easier to see for tail discounting than for Bounded MEU. If, for instance, we are considering how much we should be willing to sacrifice to reduce the probability of near-term human extinction from 0.5 to

---

[49] Versions of this idea are discussed, though not endorsed, by Buchak (2013, 73–74), Kosonen (2022, 164–178), and Beckstead and Thomas (2024, §2.3). For an argument against tail discounting (along with other forms of small-probability discounting), see Kosonen (2024).

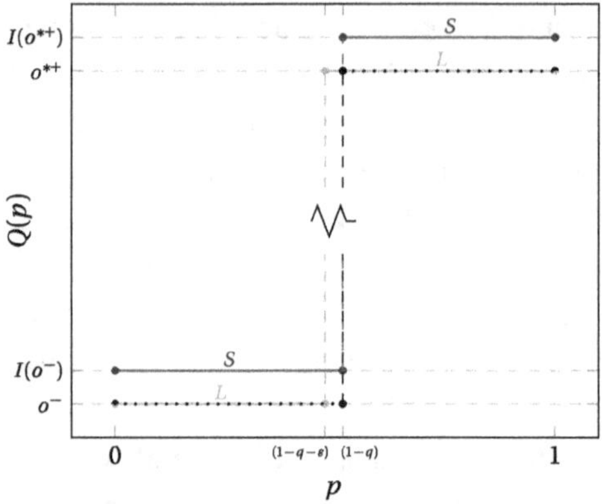



**Figure 3** Quantile functions of a baseline prospect (dotted), a safe bet ($S$) that slightly improves both possible outcomes of the baseline prospect, and a long shot ($L$) that increases the probability of the more desirable outcome by $\varepsilon$.

$0.5 - \varepsilon$, tail-discounted expected value maximization will be just as fanatical as ordinary expected value maximization.[50]

As with Bounded MEU, it's possible to devise a version of small-probability discounting that satisfies General Anti-Fanaticism. I will describe one such version, which is based on representing prospects by their *quantile functions*. For a prospect $P_i$ on a set of totally ordered outcomes, the quantile function $Q_i$ of $P_i$ is a function from probabilities to outcomes, mapping any probability $p \in (0, 1)$ to the worst outcome $o$ such that the probability of an outcome no better than $o$ is greater than or equal to $p$. Thus, for instance, $Q_i(0.5)$ gives the median outcome of $P_i$, $Q_i(0.75)$ gives the 75th percentile outcome, and so on.

Figure 3 gives an example, comparing the quantile functions of (i) a baseline prospect, (ii) a safe bet that applies an improvement to every outcome in the baseline, and (iii) a long shot that instead shifts some probability from a much worse to a much better outcome. The characteristic feature of extreme tradeoffs, in terms of quantiles, is that the quantile function of the safe bet is *slightly* greater (that is, yields a slightly better outcome) almost everywhere, while the quantile function of the long shot is greater for only a small range of $p$, but *much* greater (i.e., yields a much better outcome) at least somewhere in that range.

This concept in hand, we can now describe a version of small-probability discounting that satisfies General Anti-Fanaticism:

---

[50] For further illustrations of this point, see Kosonen (2022, Ch. 6) and Cibinel (2023). Both Kosonen and Cibinel make many of the same points about small-probability discounting in particular that Sections 6.1–6.3 have made about anti-fanaticism in general.

**Quantile Discounting** For any prospects $P_i$ and $P_j$ with quantile functions $Q_i$ and $Q_j$, if the range of quantiles where $Q_j$ exceeds $Q_i$ (formally, the Lebesgue measure of the set $\{p \in (0, 1) : Q_j(p) \succ_O Q_i(p)\}$) is below some threshold $\underline{t}$, and the range of quantiles where $Q_i$ exceeds $Q_j$ is above some further threshold $\bar{t} \leq 1 - \underline{t}$, then $P_i > P_j$.[51]

This view is, I think, the most natural and plausible form of General Anti-Fanaticism. It straightforwardly reflects and vindicates intuitions such as, for instance, that we should always prefer a sure improvement to the world over a sufficiently small reduction in the probability of existential catastrophe, no matter the baseline probability of catastrophe. But as we have seen, given No Best/Worst Outcome and Minimal Dominance, satisfying General Anti-Fanaticism must come at the cost of preference cycles. In the case illustrated by Table 4, for instance, quantile discounting will strictly prefer $P_{i+1}$ to $P_i$ for every $i < n$. Again, I don't want to totally rule out the possibility of embracing cyclicity – as described in Section 6.3, there is the mitigating circumstance that quantile discounting with a small enough probability threshold only generates very *long* cycles. But it is a steep cost to pay in order to satisfy our anti-fanatical intuitions.[52]

---

[51] This isn't a fully spelled-out decision rule. We could turn it into one by integrating it with expected value maximization, perhaps along the following lines: Let the values of the quantile function be real numbers representing the values of outcomes. Then the difference in expected value between prospects $P_i$ and $P_j$ is given by the integral of the difference of their quantile functions: $\int_0^1 Q_i(x) - Q_j(x)\, dx$. Quantile-discounted MEV might then compare $P_i$ and $P_j$ by taking this integral, while excluding one or more intervals of total length $\underline{t}$ chosen to maximize $Q_i - Q_j$, and likewise intervals of total length $\underline{t}$ chosen to maximize $Q_j - Q_i$. $P_i$ is weakly preferred to $P_j$ iff this restricted integral is weakly positive ($\geq 0$). In the example depicted in Figure 3, for instance, this rule is guaranteed to strictly prefer the safe bet as long as $\varepsilon < \underline{t}$.

[52] An alternative strategy for capturing more of our anti-fanatical intuitions within the general framework of small-probability discounting is *difference-making* tail discounting. Roughly speaking, where tail discounting ignores the most extreme outcomes of a prospect, difference-making tail discounting ignores the outcomes that *differ* most from the outcome of a baseline prospect (e.g., the prospect that results if the agent "does nothing") in the same state of nature. This form of tail discounting is discussed in Kosonen (2022, Ch. 4) and, more sympathetically, by Barrett (ms). On the other hand, Greaves et al. (2024) make a general case against any view that, like difference-making tail discounting, combines a primary concern with the difference one makes to the world with a non-neutral attitude toward risk.

I won't attempt a full discussion of the difference-making approach here, but will just make one point: Although it comes closer than simple tail discounting to capturing our anti-fanatical intuitions, I don't think it gets all the way there. Consider the case of existential risk mitigation. It might turn out that the course of human history is extremely sensitive to small changes, in such a way that every action you take has substantial – but almost exactly equal – probabilities of causing and of preventing near-term existential catastrophe. If so, then an action meant to mitigate existential risk doesn't carry a tiny probability of preventing an existential catastrophe (and thereby making a very large difference to the baseline outcome) – rather, what is tiny is the *difference* between the probability of that action preventing existential catastrophe and the

## 7 The Permissivist Synthesis

By now you're hopefully convinced that the question of how to evaluate extreme tradeoffs is a hard one. We've encountered prima facie compelling arguments for and against both fanaticism and anti-fanaticism. I'm not at all certain which of these arguments one should find convincing, as in many cases they turn on very basic and difficult questions in ethics (e.g., whether ethical "individualism" commits us to ex ante Pareto principles) or decision theory (e.g., whether dynamic inconsistency is proof of irrationality).

I find myself most convinced, however, by the dynamic consistency arguments against Narrow Fanaticism and General Anti-Fanaticism.[53] I've already explained why I'm less convinced by the arguments for Narrow Fanaticism. In this section, I'll explain why I'm unconvinced that rational preferences must be complete, and therefore unconvinced by the argument for Narrow Anti-Fanaticism described in Section 5. The combined upshot of these considerations will be the following position:

**Constrained Permissivism** It's rationally permissible to have preferences that satisfy Narrow Anti-Fanaticism, including in particular preferences that maximize the expectation of any bounded utility function that's an increasing function of value. It's also permissible to have incomplete preferences that are neither fanatical nor anti-fanatical. On the other hand, preferences that satisfy either Narrow Fanaticism or General Anti-Fanaticism are rationally impermissible.

Constrained Permissivism is a particular version of the more general permissivist alternative to fanaticism and anti-fanaticism described briefly in Section 2.4. The main purpose of this section is to explore and flesh out this position. Given that my rejection of both Narrow Fanaticism and General Anti-Fanaticism was motivated largely by considerations of dynamic consistency, I will take those considerations as my touchstone, and focus on the question of how wide a range of practical dispositions toward extreme tradeoffs are compatible with dynamic consistency. I'll end up arguing, in Sections 7.3–7.4, that it's possible for an agent to act *very much like* a Narrow Fanatic or (to a lesser extent) like a General Anti-Fanatic, while remaining dynamically consistent.

---

probability of any given alternative action preventing existential catastrophe. If the world in fact works this way, then difference-making tail discounting will do little if anything to blunt expected value arguments for existential risk mitigation, since the probability of making an astronomically large difference is not small enough to discount. But I don't think that those expectational arguments are any less counterintuitive in these circumstances.

[53] I haven't formally introduced General Fanaticism, the mirror image of General Anti-Fanaticism. But since it's a strengthening of Narrow Fanaticism, the arguments against Narrow Fanaticism apply to it as well.

Thus, at least in principle, rationality permits a fairly wide range of responses to extreme tradeoffs. (In Section 8.3, though, we'll see that rationality may be less permissive in real-world circumstances than this in-principle picture might suggest.)

A forewarning: This section will be considerably more speculative, and somewhat less formally rigorous, than the preceding sections. My aim is to sketch a picture that I find plausible, but many details of which are not yet fully worked out. I hope you'll indulge me!

## 7.1 Setup: Preference and Intention

So far we've been concerned with the rationality of various patterns of preference in the context of extreme tradeoffs. But we have largely taken the notion of *preference* for granted. To explore the implications of incomplete preferences within the constraints of dynamic consistency, though, it will be helpful to have a more definite notion of preference in mind.

The word "preference" can refer to many different phenomena: choice dispositions, judgments of objective value or choiceworthiness, feelings or inclinations toward potential objects of choice, and so on. But my view is that the sort of preferences to which norms of practical rationality apply are a kind of *intention*. The nature of intention is itself a fraught question, of course, and one that I won't try to answer here. The important features of intentions for my purposes are these: (i) Intentions concern choices that an agent expects to face or believes she might face. (ii) Intentions can be very general, and can cover particular choice situations the details of which the agent has never contemplated. For instance, a public official who has made up her mind in the abstract not to take bribes already intends, in my sense, to turn down the bribe that she will be unexpectedly offered later today. (iii) Intentions are changeable, even at the moment of choice. But part of what it is to be an agent (or at least the kind of agent we are) is that your intentions *tend* by default to persist and to be effective in action.

Consider an agent facing a sequential choice situation, described by a decision tree consisting of choice nodes and chance nodes, with each path ending in an outcome (see Section 4). The agent may have various intentions about what she will do if she reaches some future choice node: She may intend to take a particular action, or to randomize over some set of actions with certain probabilities. She may intend *not* to take some actions, without having any intentions with regard to the remaining actions, even an intention to randomize. Or she may have no intentions at all. The totality of an agent's intentions for the sequential choice situation she takes herself to be in constitute her *strategy*.

If at every choice node she intends a definite action or probability distribution over actions, we'll say that her strategy is *complete*. A complete strategy that intends a definite action at each choice node is *pure*; one that sometimes intends to randomize is *mixed*.

A *terminal* choice node is one that's not followed by any other choice nodes. Each action at a terminal choice node can be associated with a prospect: the probability distribution over outcomes that results from that action, given any succeeding chance nodes. Similarly, at any node in a sequential choice situation, any complete strategy can be associated with a prospect: the probability distribution over outcomes that results from following that strategy, starting from that node. Say that a prospect $P_i$ is *available* at a choice node if there's some available strategy that, from the agent's perspective at that node, would yield $P_i$.

An ideally rational agent should, in general, entertain the possibility of finding herself in a wide range of future choice situations. That is, her decision tree should be very large, containing a wide variety of possible subtrees (even if nearly all of them have extremely low probability), including for instance terminal choices between any given pair of prospects. For an agent whose intentions cover a sufficiently rich set of future eventualities, we can define a preference relation on prospects in terms of those intentions. We can say that she *strictly prefers $P_i$ to $P_j$* if she intends, at any terminal choice node it's possible to reach given her intentions where both $P_i$ and $P_j$ are available, not to choose $P_j$. She is *indifferent* between $P_i$ and $P_j$ if for any prospect $P_k$, $P_i > P_k$ if and only if $P_j > P_k$, and $P_k > P_i$ if and only if $P_k > P_j$. And she *lacks a preference* between $P_i$ and $P_j$ if neither of these relations holds.

These definitions immediately imply what is often taken to be the defining characteristic of preference gaps: an insensitivity to small improvements or worsenings. If an agent lacks a preference between $P_i$ and $P_j$, then there must be some other prospect $P_k$ that she strictly prefers to $P_i$ but not to $P_j$, or strictly prefers to $P_j$ but not to $P_i$, or strictly disprefers to $P_i$ but not to $P_j$, or strictly disprefers to $P_j$ but not to $P_i$.

## 7.2 Incomplete Preferences and Sequential Choice

This understanding of preference in terms of conditional intentions gives us more expressive power in describing a permissive picture of rationality. In this subsection, I'll describe how rational requirements on intention can allow an agent with incomplete preferences to avoid sequential irrationality. The next two subsections will explore just how constraining those requirements are with respect to extreme tradeoffs – how far they allow an agent to go in the direction of Narrow Fanaticism on the one hand, or General Anti-Fanaticism on the other.

Permissivist views hold that rationality permits more than one set of attitudes in risky choice situations. But *Constrained* Permissivism holds that this permission is not all-encompassing. I will assume that rationality requires at least that an agent avoid stochastically dominated prospects. In the framework of intentions for sequential choice situations, this prohibition takes the form of at least two requirements. Here's the first (the second will be introduced shortly):

**Avoidance of Dominated Actions (ADA)** Suppose that, at choice node $N$, every pure strategy that allows the agent to reach choice node $N'$ and includes an intention to choose act $A$ at $N'$ is stochastically dominated at $N$. Then it's rationally required at $N$ that the agent's intentions rule out choosing $A$ at $N'$ – either by ruling out that she reaches $N'$, or by including an intention not to choose $A$ at $N'$.[54]

Given the definition of strict preference above, ADA turns out to imply that an agent must strictly prefer stochastically dominant prospects. (That is, it implies the strict part of the principle of Stochastic Dominance introduced in Section 4.)

An agent with incomplete preferences, if she respects ADA, will avoid the standard forms of dynamic inconsistency associated with incompleteness. (I don't have a proof that ADA is sufficient to avoid *any* money pump for incompleteness, though I conjecture that it is.) The standard dynamic consistency objection to incomplete preferences is illustrated in Figure 4. In this sequential choice situation, we have three possible outcomes: $P_1$, $P_1^-$, and $P_2$. We assume that the agent lacks a preference between $P_1$ and $P_2$, and that $P_1^-$ is strictly dispreferred to $P_1$ but not to $P_2$. Let's further assume that $P_1^-$ is

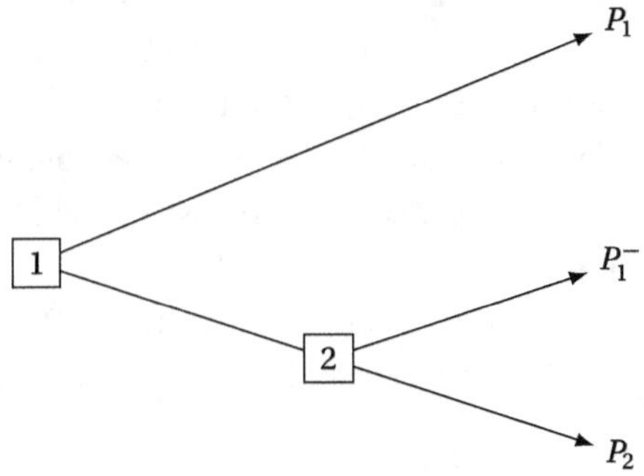

**Figure 4** A money pump for incomplete preferences

---

[54] This is closely related to the principle of Non-Domination introduced in Section 4. The main difference is that, whereas Non-Domination is a description of rational *behavior*, ADA is a normative requirement on rational *intentions*.

stochastically dominated by $P_1$. (Standardly, $P_1^-$ would be understood as $P_1$ with some "souring," e.g., the loss of \$1, that makes it both statewise and stochastically dominated by $P_1$.) The worry is that, because the agent does not strictly prefer $P_1$ to $P_2$, she might go down at node 1; but then, because she does not strictly prefer $P_2$ to $P_1^-$, she might go up at node 2. She would thereby end up with a prospect inferior to one that she could have had at the outset.

Note that, unlike the money-pump argument against fanaticism in Section 4.2 (and the argument for Acyclicity alluded to in Section 6.3), this money pump is "non-forcing": the argument is not that the agent's preferences, together with principles of rational choice, *require* her to make a sequence of choices that leads to an inferior prospect. It's merely that her preferences seem to *allow* a sequence of choices that leads to an inferior prospect.[55] It's open to us, therefore, without contradicting any principle of rationality we have so far affirmed, to argue that rationality will allow an agent with incomplete preferences to reliably avoid this trap.

ADA serves precisely this purpose. An agent who satisfies ADA will, at node 1 in Figure 4, either intend to choose $P_1$ at node 1 or else intend not to choose $P_1^-$ at node 2: There is only one pure strategy that both allows the agent to reach node 2 and includes an intention to go up at that node (namely, "down at 1, up at 2"), and this strategy is stochastically dominated since it yields prospect $P_1^-$, while an available alternative strategy (viz, either strategy that includes "up at 1") yields the stochastically dominant prospect $P_1$. This means that, as long as the agent's intentions don't change and she acts according to those intentions, she will avoid ending up with $P_1^-$. (And this is compatible with her having no preference between $P_2$ on the one hand and $P_1/P_1^-$ on the other: She may have no intentions with respect to these prospects beyond the conditional intention that, *if* she goes down at node 1, then she'll go down at node 2.) This doesn't *guarantee* that she'll avoid $P_1^-$, because her intentions might change between her first choice and her second. And I don't think that there is any rational prohibition on changing your intentions. But having complete preferences or intentions wouldn't shield an agent against the risk of ending up with an inferior prospect as a result of preference change either.

In fact, given our definition of strict preference, ADA has the following interesting implication: Suppose prospect $P_1$ is available at choice node $N$,

---

[55] Gustafsson (2022, §3) has a clever argument that incompleteness makes you vulnerable to *forcing* money pumps. But this argument depends on a questionable principle ("precautionary backward induction"; 34) whose main motivation is the avoidance of *non*-forcing money pumps. Insofar as we have a way to avoid non-forcing money pumps, the motivation for this principle is undermined, and with it the forcing argument.

only if the agent does not choose action $A$. And suppose that any pure strategy that chooses $A$ yields either a prospect stochastically dominated by $P_1$, or else $P_2$, which is not so dominated. Then, if the agent's intentions satisfy ADA before making her choice at $N$, and she chooses $A$ at $N$, and her intentions don't change, then she will subsequently have a strict preference for $P_2$ over *any* prospect $P_1^-$ that is stochastically dominated by $P_1$. That is, if her preferences satisfy ADA then she will intend, at any terminal choice node that can be reached by choosing $A$, that it's possible to reach given her intentions, and where both $P_2$ and $P_1^-$ are available, not to choose $P_1^-$.[56] Thus, for instance, in Figure 4, even if the agent starts off with no preference between $P_1$ and $P_2$ and no intention about whether to go up or down at node 1, she must intend that *if* she goes down at node 1 (turning down $P_1$ to put herself in a situation where the only option not stochastically dominated by $P_1$ is $P_2$), she will subsequently choose $P_2$ over any prospect stochastically dominated by $P_1$. Intentions that satisfy ADA, in other words, have the effect of *filling in* gaps in an agent's preferences based on her choices. This is what allows an agent with incomplete preferences to avoid sequential irrationality.

## 7.3 Almost Fanaticism

What does a permissivist picture constrained by principles like ADA imply about rational behavior in the face of extreme tradeoffs? How far is it possible to go in the direction of fanaticism or anti-fanaticism, within such constraints?

Let's consider the fanatical direction first. In particular, let's consider how close an agent can permissibly come to the paradigmatically fanatical decision rule of expected value maximization, within constraints that rule out dynamic inconsistency. Recall the anti-fanatical money pump from Section 4.2 (p. 31): An agent has the chance to receive the St. Petersburg-like prospect $\text{Blue}^{++}$. But unless she trades it, *before* learning its outcome, for the stochastically dominated prospect $\text{Blue}^+$, she will be offered a chance, *after* learning its outcome, to trade that outcome for the prospect Green. Although Green is stochastically

---

[56] Deriving this implication requires the assumption that any future choice node that it's *possible* for an agent to reach given her intentions, she *will* reach with non-zero probability. That in particular requires the probability distributions associated with chance nodes to be discrete, without probability-zero branches. This is somewhat tricky to reconcile with the assumption that the agent's decision tree contains a sufficiently rich set of subtrees (e.g., terminal pairwise choices between any pair of prospects). The best way I know how to do this, at the moment, is to restrict the domains of outcomes, prospects, and decision subtrees based on *computability*, i.e., to consider only the countable sets of outcomes, prospects, and decision subtrees a description of which can be output by a Turing machine. The set of computable decision subtrees is countable, so that the agent can assign non-zero probability to ending up in any of them, but is rich enough to include for instance terminal choices between any finite set of computable prospects.

dominated by both Blue$^{++}$ and Blue$^+$, it is preferred (in virtue of the agent's fanaticism) to every possible *outcome* of Blue$^{++}$. There are two things we need to avoid in this situation. One is the agent choosing Blue$^+$ at the first choice node. This is ruled out by ADA: Any strategy that includes an intention to go up (choosing Blue$^+$) at the first choice node is stochastically dominated by the alternative strategy of picking Blue$^{++}$ and sticking with it. Since at the initial node the agent's intentions can't rule out that she reaches that very node, ADA requires that she intend not to go up.

The second thing we want to avoid is that, after choosing Blue$^{++}$ and learning its outcome, the agent switches to the inferior prospect Green regardless of that outcome. Here no single action that the agent takes is stochastically dominated – it is only the totality of her intentions that constitute a stochastically dominated strategy. To guard against this risk, therefore, we need another constraint on rational intentions:

**Avoidance of Dominated Strategies (ADS)** It's rationally required of an agent at a choice node $N$ that her strategy (the totality of her intentions for potential future choice nodes) not be such that any completion of it yields a prospect stochastically dominated by another prospect available at $N$.

ADS implies that, at the initial node, one must not intend to turn down Blue$^+$, but then switch to Green regardless of the outcome of the blue coin tosses, since the prospect yielded by that strategy is stochastically dominated by other prospects available at that node (namely, the prospects Blue$^+$ and Blue$^{++}$). In fact, ADS implies that there must be some $n$ such that, for any $m \geq n$, one does *not* intend to turn down $o_m$ in favor of Green.

Given our definition of preference, and given that an agent cannot rule out eventually being faced with a situation like the St. Petersburg money pump, this conclusion rules out full-blown expected value maximization. For an agent's preferences to satisfy MEV, by our definition, would mean that she always intends not to take an action with less expected value when an action with greater expected value is available. And that would mean intending not to stick with the outcome of Blue$^{++}$, regardless of what it is, which violates ADS.

The fact that our agent doesn't intend to choose Green at every opportunity means that there is at least some outcome $o_n$ that she *might*, as far as her intentions are concerned, choose over Green. Moreover, suppose she anticipates that if she turns down Green in favor of $o_n$, she will be offered a further option to switch to a prospect that has greater expected value than $o_n$ but is stochastically dominated by Green – for instance, the prospect $\langle o^{n+1}, 2^{-(n+1)}, o^- \rangle$.

By ADA, she must intend at the initial choice node not to make this trade if she's confronted with it, since any strategy that involves making the trade is stochastically dominated by an otherwise identical strategy that chooses Green over $o_n$. Thus, she must intend (at least in certain respects) to "stick with" the choice she makes after seeing the blue coin flips, which can entail a definite intention not to make other expected-value-maximizing choices in future.

But a permissivist picture constrained by ADA and ADS still allows an agent to act *very much like* a Narrow Fanatic. To begin with, one easy way of satisfying these and other dynamic consistency constraints is to be a bounded expected utility maximizer. The only constraint on such an agent's utility function is that it must assign greater utility to better outcomes (since otherwise it would violate Minimal Dominance and hence Stochastic Dominance, and the implied intentions would violate ADA/ADS). This allows an agent, in a sense, to act arbitrarily like a Narrow Fanatic, simply by adopting a utility function whose bounds are sufficiently extreme, and that is linear or sufficiently close to linear over a large enough interval of value. For instance, a bounded expected utility maximizer's utility function might be precisely linear with respect to value for all outcomes better than $n$ billion-year lives of hellish suffering and worse than $n$ billion-year lives of bliss, for some incomprehensibly vast $n$ (say, Graham's number).

But it's possible to go a bit further even than this, within the intention-based framework I've outlined. It is rationally permissible for an agent to intend always to take the action with greater expected value unless and until she is faced with an option with infinite expected value – and more specifically, with a situation like the St. Petersburg money pump beyond which her intention to maximize expected value must be limited.[57] Where a bounded expected utility maximizer has formed a definite intention not to maximize expected value beyond some point (when the outcomes involved are sufficiently extreme that they exceed the linear or nearly linear intermediate portion of her utility function), an agent who has incomplete preferences with respect to extreme tradeoffs has made no such precommitment. Though she does not intend to

---

[57] I'm glossing over an important complication here: If an agent thinks she *might*, with non-zero probability, be faced at some point with a prospect like the St. Petersburg game with infinite expected value, and choose it, then none of the actions available to her right now will have finite expected value – that chance of a future infinity infects all her present choices (Hájek and Smithson, 2012). (The same goes for prospects with negative infinite or undefined expected value.) In this case, she can't decide what to do based on expected value in the ordinary sense. But there are various natural extensions of MEV to handle prospects without finite expectations, that would allow such an agent, if her situation is reasonably well-behaved (e.g., if the prospects available to her *differ* only finitely) to evaluate her options in a way very much in the spirit of MEV (see for instance Colyvan, 2008; Easwaran, 2008; Wilkinson, 2025).

take her penchant for fanatical expected value maximization to *any* extreme, she leaves it open just how far she is willing to take it.

## 7.4 Almost Anti-Fanaticism?

Now consider the opposite question: How far in the direction of anti-fanaticism is it possible to go, within the guardrails of Constrained Permissivism?

Just as the view developed in this section rules out full-fledged Narrow Fanaticism, so it rules out General Anti-Fanaticism (given No Best/Worst Outcome). We saw that ADA implies the strict part of Stochastic Dominance, which in turn implies Minimal Dominance. And the understanding of preferences described in Section 7.1 makes Acyclicity almost tautological. To strictly prefer $P_i$ to $P_j$, recall, means that you intend not to choose $P_j$ at any terminal choice node where $P_i$ is available. If, then, you have the preferences $P_i > P_j > P_k > P_i$, what do you intend to do in a straight choice between those three prospects? You must intend to choose none of your available options. Such an intention may be simply impossible, but at minimum it involves a sort of practical contradiction (since your intentions are jointly incompatible) which rationality ought to rule out. Thus, on the understanding of preference we're working with, cyclic preferences are either impossible or irrational.

As we've seen, Constrained Permissivism leaves open the option of simply being a bounded expected utility maximizer, and thereby satisfying *Narrow Anti-Fanaticism*. And just as a bounded expected utility maximizer can go arbitrarily far in the direction of fanaticism, by choosing a utility function that is linear or nearly linear over some arbitrarily wide range of outcomes, so she can go arbitrarily far in the opposite direction, making her utility arbitrarily close to flat outside some central range of outcomes and making that central range arbitrarily small, as long as she always assigns greater utility to better outcomes. But we've also seen (in Section 6.4) that this won't be enough to fully satisfy our anti-fanatical intuitions; for instance, the bounded expected utility maximizer must, in some circumstances, prefer arbitrarily small shifts in probability from one outcome to another over saving 1000 lives for sure.

But as with the would-be fanatic, Constrained Permissivism opens up other possibilities for the would-be anti-fanatic. While Bounded MEU requires her to precommit to the circumstances in which she will prefer a long shot over a safe bet, an agent with incomplete preferences can avoid such commitments. With respect to a sequence of prospects that a General Anti-Fanatic might rank cyclically, for instance, she could strictly prefer the safe bet to the long shot for many pairs of consecutive prospects, while maintaining preference gaps for other pairs, leaving it open which trade in the cycle she would refuse.

There is a sense, though, in which the constraints of sequential rationality don't let us get *as* close to full anti-fanaticism as to full fanaticism: Take the preference relation $\succsim_{ev}$ that ranks prospects by expected value. This relation of course satisfies Narrow Fanaticism (if value is unbounded), as well as any natural generalization of fanaticism to the context of uncertain baseline prospects. Constrained Permissivism allows an agent to rank any *finite* set of prospects that are ranked by expected value in a way that exactly agrees with that ranking. (For instance, it's possible to find a bounded utility function that yields the same ranking of that set.) One's preferences can't *always* agree with $\succsim_{ev}$, on pain of sequential irrationality, but there's no particular point at which they must stop. But the same can't be said for any preference relation $\succsim_{gaf}$ that satisfies General Anti-Fanaticism. Given No Best/Worst Outcome, any such relation must either violate Minimal Dominance or include finite cycles of strict preference. And in either case, we can find a finite set of prospects $S$ such that no rational preference relation can fully agree with $\succsim_{gaf}$ in the ranking of $S$. In this sense, Constrained Permissivism allows one to go farther in the direction of fanaticism than in the direction of anti-fanaticism.

## 7.5 Summing Up

We began our discussion of fanaticism, in Section 2, with two examples that were meant to drive home the counterintuitiveness of fanatical reasoning, as typified by expected value maximization. The conclusion we have reached is that this intuitive resistance to fanaticism holds at least two grains of truth: First, we are not rationally required to be risk-neutral expected value maximizers in any given situation – we are permitted to display a wider range of attitudes toward risk in general, and toward small differences in the probabilities of extreme outcomes in particular. It is rationally permissible, for instance, to be a bounded expected utility maximizer. Second, we are sometimes rationally required to *deviate* from risk-neutral expected value maximization – for example, by not preferring a St. Petersburg game to all its possible outcomes. At the same time, our anti-fanatical intuitions cannot be *fully* satisfied, without committing ourselves to irrationally cyclic preferences. I've argued for a middle road, which aims to permit an agent to be as fanatical or anti-fanatical as she likes within constraints that help her avoid ending up with dominated prospects.

This intermediate view has costs relative to both fanaticism and anti-fanaticism. Compared to fanaticism, it has to deny Anteriority and similar prima facie compelling principles. Compared to anti-fanaticism, it has to give up some common intuitions – for instance, the intuition that it is positively irrational to turn down certainty of a very good outcome for a $10^{-100}$ chance at an *astronomically* good outcome. Moreover, despite the arguments in Section 7.2, one might still find Completeness compelling. Finally, one might worry that permissivism permits too much, leaving us with too little normative guidance with respect to extreme tradeoffs and risky choices more generally.

In the next section, however, we'll examine a surprising argument that *in practice*, any agent with preferences that satisfy Stochastic Dominance should nearly always act like an expected value maximizer, even in some contexts that look intuitively like extreme tradeoffs. This argument, if successful, will move the permissivist picture closer to intuition in some respects and further from intuition in others, and will serve at least to mitigate worries about practical action guidance.

## 8 Fanaticism, Anti-Fanaticism, and Permissivism in Practice

We've now completed our theoretical investigation of fanaticism, anti-fanaticism, and permissivism. In this final section, we'll turn from theory to practice. Whereas we have thus far been asking how much weight one should be willing to give *in principle* to small differences in the probabilities of extreme outcomes, we will now ask to what extent *in practice* the choices of a rational, morally motivated agent should be influenced by such small probability differences. The answers to these two questions can easily come apart: For instance, it could be that MEV is the correct principle of rationality, but also that, in the choices actually faced by real-world agents, safe bets almost always carry greater expected value than long shots. On the other hand, it could be that quantile-discounted MEV is the correct principle of rationality, but the threshold for rational discounting is so small (say, $10^{-1000}$) that discounting is almost practically inert, and the ranking of prospects is often determined by probability differences that are intuitively quite small (say, $10^{-100}$).

To keep the discussion manageable, we'll focus on just one kind of practical situation: *unconstrained altruistic prioritization*. This is the situation of an agent who wants to do as much good as possible with some limited resource, and faces no major external constraints on the ends to which she devotes that resource. (The resource in question could for instance be money, as in the case of philanthropic giving, or time, as in the case of altruistically motivated career choice.) Our question will be: Should such agents, in practice, primarily pursue strategies that have a relatively good chance of making a modest positive difference to the world, or strategies that have a very small chance of making a very large difference?

Sections 8.1–8.2 will consider what MEV says about this question: For a would-be altruist deciding which projects to focus her limited resources on, how often are long shots expected-value-maximizing? Section 8.1 will consider whether it's sufficiently prima facie plausible that altruistically motivated agents can have extreme positive impacts on the world that we should expect long-shot altruistic projects aiming for such impacts to carry significant expected value. Section 8.2 will examine, as a case study, recent debates over the comparative priority of *existential risk mitigation* versus cause areas like global public health that offer more immediate and certain benefits. I'll argue it's at least very plausible that ambitious altruistic projects like existential risk mitigation are often expected-value-maximizing, even when their probability of success is small, so that MEV is significantly fanatical in practice as well as in principle.

That investigation serves a double purpose. First, how fanatical MEV is in practice constitutes a worthwhile question in its own right; and since MEV is the paradigmatic form of fanaticism, it tells us something about the practical implications that may follow if one is persuaded by the arguments for fanaticism in Section 3. But second, I'll argue in Section 8.3 that under real-world circumstances, *any* plausible theory of rational choice – specifically, any theory that satisfies Stochastic Dominance – must generally agree with MEV in practice. This is because, once we take account of our "background uncertainty" about sources of value in the world unaffected by our choices, expected-value-maximizing options very often turn out to stochastically dominate their expectationally inferior alternatives. Thus, in many cases, the practical implications of MEV *are also* implied by any reasonable form of fanaticism, anti-fanaticism, or permissivism. In particular, the Constrained Permissivist view defended in the last section will share much of MEV's penchant for long shots in the context of altruistic prioritization – though, I'll argue, it can still escape the most extreme and implausible instances of real-world expected value fanaticism.

Throughout this section we'll make a substantive assumption that we haven't made so far: we'll assume an *impartial additive* theory of value. This means that the overall value of an outcome is the sum of degrees of value realized at each value location (e.g., the value of each welfare subject's life), with all locations given equal weight. And we will understand MEV as ranking prospects by the expectation of that additive value function.

## 8.1 Altruistic Long Shots

How fanatical is MEV in practice, in the context of altruistic prioritization? That is, how often does it recommend long shots over safe bets, and how extreme are the long shots it recommends?

Real-world altruists have some fairly attractive "safe bets" available to them. For instance, the charity evaluator GiveWell studies the cost-effectiveness of various philanthropically funded public health programs in developing countries, and finds that several such programs are able to save lives at an average cost of a few thousand dollars. (As of January 2025, the most cost-effective program in GiveWell's estimation is Helen Keller Intl's vitamin A supplementation program, with an estimated cost of ~\$3500 per life saved (GiveWell, 2025).) A philanthropist aiming to do as much good as possible with her money could choose to fund these programs; someone aiming to do good in her career could work for an organization that implements them.[58]

Are there even better opportunities to be had, though, pursuing altruistic long shots – projects with only a small chance of success, but extreme positive impact if they succeed? One way to think about this question, in expected value terms, is to ask how the probability of success in an altruistic endeavor varies with its level of ambition. Saving 100 million lives is harder than saving 100 – but how much harder is it, as measured by probability of success? If it's 10 million times harder, then, at least prima facie, it looks like a worse bet in expected value terms; if it's only 100,000 times harder, then it looks like a better bet.

It's hard to get much empirical traction on this very general question. But there are some scraps of evidence to suggest that extreme positive impacts on the world, while unlikely, are not *astronomically* unlikely. For instance, there are plausible historical examples of single individuals having such impacts: Norman Borlaug's work to increase agricultural productivity has been estimated to have saved more than one billion people from starvation (Avery, 2011); Victor Zhdanov has been credited with bringing about the World Health Organization's successful campaign to eradicate smallpox (Irlam, 2023), a disease estimated to have killed 300 million people in the twentieth century alone (Henderson, 2011). More systematically, analyses of published cost-effectiveness estimates for public health interventions and other social programs generally find that the cost-effectiveness of different programs follows a

---

[58] Of course, there are many uncertainties about the impact of even the most tried-and-true philanthropic programs. You cannot, for instance, be certain that the effect of donating \$3500 to Helen Keller Intl will be a single life saved and nothing else. Even the best cost-effectiveness estimates are only an average, they involve many assumptions that are open to dispute, and they don't try to measure a plethora of potentially important indirect effects. What's important for our purposes is that one might reasonably believe that the overall expected value of donating to a charity like Helen Keller Intl is in the neighborhood of one life saved per \$3500 donated, and that this expectation is not primarily driven by a tiny probability of an astronomically large impact.

heavy-tailed distribution (e.g., log-normal or power law), meaning that extreme values – programs vastly more cost-effective than the typical program – show up with nontrivial frequency (Ord, 2013; Todd, 2023). This provides at least weak evidence that the probability of success in an altruistic endeavor does not drop off too precipitously with its level of ambition.

Even if extreme impacts show up with significant frequency, ex post, that doesn't necessarily mean that small differences in the probability of extreme impacts play a significant role in ex ante comparisons of expected value. It could be, on the one hand, that opportunities for extreme impact are highly foreseeable when they arise, so that the actions giving rise to such impacts are not long shots but rather especially attractive safe bets. On the other hand, perhaps extreme impacts are almost entirely *un*predictable: All philanthropic projects carry a nontrivial probability of doing extreme good, but alternative projects with the same resource budget don't *differ* significantly in their likelihood of extreme impact, so that the possibility of extreme impact plays little role in expected value comparisons. But neither of these patterns seems especially plausible. It seems more plausible that some philanthropic alternatives are several times more likely than others to have extreme positive impacts, though the differences in probability are still small in absolute terms. For instance, a career as a cancer researcher or as an advocate for nuclear arms reduction seem much more likely than most altruistically motivated careers to result in extreme positive impact (on the order of, say, millions of lives saved), though the absolute probability of such impact is still small. If there are altruistic long shots whose probability of extreme impact is small but not vanishingly small, and many times larger than that of safer alternatives, then we should expect those differences in probability of extreme impact to carry substantial weight in expected value comparisons, potentially giving long shots greater overall expected value than safe bets.

## 8.2 Case Study: Existential Risk

The reasoning in the last section is only suggestive – it suggests that extreme altruistic impacts, though improbable, may be probable enough to carry significant weight in expected value comparisons. But we can learn more about the practical proclivities of MEV in the context of extreme tradeoffs by examining a particular type of altruistic long shot: efforts to mitigate risks of extreme catastrophes like human extinction. As we saw in Section 1, authors like Bostrom (2003, 2013) and Ord (2020) have argued on expected value grounds that avoiding existential catastrophe should be an overwhelming practical priority in present circumstances, even in contexts where the effect we can have on the probability of catastrophe is very small. Many altruistically motivated individuals and philanthropic organizations have found these arguments persuasive. The question of how to prioritize between existential risk mitigation and "safer" altruistic objectives like global public health is therefore one where the abstract problem of how to handle extreme tradeoffs takes on great practical importance.

The expected value of existential risk mitigation efforts depends, to a reasonable approximation, on three factors: First, what is the "baseline" probability of a near-term existential catastrophe (say, in the next century)? Second, how much can that probability be reduced for a given investment of resources? Third, how bad would an existential catastrophe be, in expectation?

On the question of baseline probabilities, estimates vary enormously. On the pessimistic end, Rees (2003) argued for a 50% probability that humanity would not survive the twenty-first century. Ord (2020, 167) estimates the probability of an existential catastrophe in the next hundred years at one-in-six. Perhaps the most systematic effort to quantify existential risk comes from Karger et al. (2023), who brought together 80 domain experts on potential existential risks and 89 "superforecasters" with track records of predictive accuracy on near-term forecasting questions. Interestingly, even after an extended exchange of arguments between study participants, risk estimates varied significantly between these two groups: the median domain expert estimated a 6% chance of human extinction before 2100, while the median superforecaster estimated only a 1% chance.

Next, how much can we reduce existential risk, for a given investment of resources? Published answers to this question are harder to find, and arguably involve an even larger element of subjective guesswork. Millett and Snyder-Beattie (2017) estimate that $250 billion spent on biosecurity measures could reduce the risk of human extinction from accidental or intentional misuse of biotechnology in the next century by at least 1% from its baseline level. More optimistically, Todd (2017) estimates that $100 billion spent on reducing extinction risk could achieve an *absolute* risk reduction of 1% (e.g., reducing total risk from 4% to 3%).

Finally, how bad would a catastrophe on the scale of human extinction be? The standard way of answering that question is to ask how many human lives (or nonhuman lives of at least similar value) our civilization might ultimately support if we avoid existential catastrophe and survive as long as the relevant physical constraints allow. For instance, if humanity remains permanently Earthbound and limited to roughly current population levels, but survives as long as the Earth remains habitable, our future population might amount to

~$10^{17}$ individuals.[59] With more ambitious assumptions, however, the numbers can get *much* larger. For instance, Bostrom (2003, 2013) estimates that if we manage to settle most of the accessible universe, and make efficient use of its resources, our civilization could ultimately support $10^{52}$ human lives worth of subjective experience in digital form.

Taking these numbers at face value suggests that the expectational case for existential risk mitigation efforts is very strong, even when those efforts make only a tiny difference to the probability of existential catastrophe. For instance, take the lower estimate of baseline risk from Karger et al. (the super-forecaster estimate of 1%), assume that risks from biotechnology account for only 10% of that risk, and take the lower-bound cost-effectiveness estimate from Millett and Snyder-Beattie of a 1% relative reduction in extinction risks from biotechnology for \$250 billion. Further assume that spending to reduce these risks has constant marginal returns.[60] We then find that \$1 spent on reducing extinction risks from biotechnology at the current margin reduces the probability of existential catastrophe over the next century by $4 \times 10^{-17}$. If the value of averting existential catastrophe is equivalent to $10^{17}$ human lives, then the expected cost-effectiveness of existential risk reduction is about 4 lives per dollar spent. This greatly exceeds any credible cost-effectiveness estimates for more ordinary philanthropic projects, like public health programs in developing countries. Thus, even on what look like conservative assumptions across the board, there seems to be a strong expected value case for prioritizing long-shot existential risk mitigation efforts over safer philanthropic bets.

A number of serious objections can be raised to these back-of-the-envelope calculations, however, which exemplify more general worries about expected value reasoning in the context of extreme tradeoffs. Let's focus on the estimation of the stakes of existential catastrophe. Is it really plausible that the difference in expected value between humanity surviving versus not surviving the next century is on the order of $10^{17}$ human lives (let alone $10^{52}$)? As various critics have emphasized (especially Thorstad, 2023, 2024), there are good reasons doubt these numbers. For instance, even if humanity survives the twenty-first century (perhaps thanks to your altruistic efforts!), we might still go extinct in the twenty-second or the twenty-third, or... If there is a nontrivial, ineliminable risk of existential catastrophe in all future centuries, the

---

[59] This assumes a population of 10 billion individuals persisting for the next billion years, with individual lifespans of 100 years.

[60] That's a conservative assumption with respect to the marginal cost-effectiveness of existential risk reduction, since we would normally expect diminishing returns, which would make current marginal returns higher than average returns on a large investment.

probability that we survive for millions or billions of years might be extremely low even conditional on surviving the next century, and so the expected value of surviving the next century may be only modest. For another thing, even if we survive for a very long time, it's not obvious that our long-term population will be anywhere close to our theoretical carrying capacity (Spears and Geruso, 2025). These concerns suggest a general lesson that extreme estimates of the stakes of a decision are a natural result of over-simple models, e.g., models that assume that some local event (like human survival or extinction in the twenty-first century) will have a uniform, predictable effect across a very wide region of space and time. Adding nuance to our models is likely to generate a regression toward the mean, deflating rather than inflating extreme estimates of the stakes of our choices.

There's a plausible reply to these worries within the framework of expected value maximization, however, that trades on MEV's embrace of fanaticism: Even if the simple models that yield extreme estimates of the stakes of existential catastrophe are *unlikely* to be correct, even a small chance that they're correct is enough to yield enormous expected value. Consider, for instance, the issue of exogenous extinction risks in future centuries. Those most concerned with existential risk often claim that we're living in a "time of perils," a moment when existential risks are unusually high (Sagan, 1994). If we survive the next century or millennium, reach technological maturity, achieve greater individual and collective wisdom, and spread our eggs across more baskets by establishing self-sustaining settlements on other planets, then the per-century probability of existential catastrophe may thereafter be quite low, and there is at least a nontrivial chance that our civilization will survive and thrive for billions of years to come. The time of perils hypothesis is of course speculative, and open to criticism (Thorstad, 2023). But it's also intuitively natural,[61] and can be supported by substantial theoretical arguments (Trammell and Aschenbrenner, 2024). It would seem overconfident to assign this hypothesis a probability less than, say, 0.1%. Likewise, the hypothesis that if we avoid extinction, we will make the most of our collective future (e.g., by settling the accessible part of the universe and using its resources in whatever way produces most value) is certainly open to doubt, but deserves nontrivial credence. (Among other considerations, whatever one takes the best future for humanity to look like, its being best is in itself a significant reason to expect our descendants to pursue it.)

---

[61] In particular, it's natural to think that the per-century risk of human extinction has been very low for nearly all of human history, and has become substantial only in the last century. And if that's true, then it seems about as natural to hypothesize that our current situation is a one-time aberration as that it represents a new permanent status quo.

And assigning even a very small probability to the time of perils hypothesis combined with an astronomical estimate of the ultimate value of human civilization is enough to make the stakes of existential catastrophe enormous in expected value terms. For instance, assigning even $10^{-18}$ (one in a billion billion) probability to the conjecture that, conditional on surviving the next century, we will achieve a future on the order of Bostrom's $10^{52}$ life equivalents implies that the expected value of avoiding extinction this century is at least equivalent to $10^{34}$ lives – far more than the $10^{17}$ assumed in the naive argument above.[62]

Once again, there's a general lesson here about fanatical applications of expected value reasoning: Higher-order uncertainties about important terms like the value of surviving the next century tend to push the stakes up rather than down, and strengthen the case for long shots over safe bets. In particular, this is true when our uncertainties are "logarithmic," spanning many orders of magnitude of similarly plausible estimates. As a toy illustration, suppose your best estimate of the number of future humans is $10^{12}$, but you think this estimate could easily be off by an order of magnitude in either direction, assigning equal credence to $10^{11}$ and $10^{13}$. The average of these two numbers is greater than $10^{12}$, and so this uncertainty will push the expected number of future humans to be higher than your initial point estimate rather than lower. The more extreme your uncertainties, the more extreme the effect, as long as your uncertainties are roughly symmetric on a logarithmic scale.

The preceding discussion is, of course, far from comprehensive, let alone decisive. But I have tried at least to sketch a case that MEV's penchant for fanaticism is not merely theoretical. We face choices that *might* have extremely high stakes, for instance when we decide what charities to support or how to spend our careers. And when we do our best to put numbers on the stakes, and on the relevant probabilities, it may well turn out that very small differences we can make to the probabilities of very high-stakes outcomes are the decisive factors in expected value calculations.

## 8.3 Background Uncertainty

So far in this section, I've sketched a case that in at least one significant real-world context, small differences in the probabilities of extreme outcomes play a decisive role in determining the comparative expected value of our options. In the context of altruistic prioritization, an expected value maximizer should plausibly be guided by these small probability differences. But does this

---

[62] I develop an argument to this effect in more detail in Tarsney (2023), especially Section 6.1.

conclusion, if correct, have any relevance to non-expected-value-maximizers – for instance, to someone who accepts a permissivist picture like the one I sketched in the last section? In this final subsection, I'll make the case that it does.

There are two essential elements to this case. One is the principle of Stochastic Dominance introduced and defended in Section 4.1. As I said in the last section, I believe that even the permissivist should endorse this substantive constraint on the rational ranking of prospects. The second essential element is the phenomenon of *background uncertainty*. Background uncertainty (or *background risk*) is an agent's uncertainty about sources of value that are unaffected by her present choices. In the context of an impartial additive theory of value, it can be identified more specifically with uncertainty about local outcomes at unaffected value locations. This might include past humans and animals on Earth, distant aliens, and any present or future welfare subjects who, though affectable in principle, are known to be unaffected by one's present choice. Given this division, a prospect can be understood as a probability distribution over ordered pairs of a "foreground outcome" (the outcome at affected value locations) and a "background outcome" (the outcome at unaffected locations). The implied probability distribution over foreground outcomes alone can be called the *foreground prospect*, and the distribution over background outcomes the *background prospect*. Because it's unaffectable, all available prospects in a given choice situation share the same background prospect.

In Tarsney (2025b), I prove two results concerning the implications of Stochastic Dominance under background uncertainty.[63] The first result shows that, if one foreground prospect has greater expected value than another, it will become stochastically dominant when combined with sufficient background uncertainty – that is, the overall prospect with the expectationally superior foreground component will stochastically dominate the overall prospect with the expectationally inferior foreground component.[64] This means that any decision theory satisfying Stochastic Dominance will require an agent to choose the option whose foreground prospect maximizes expected value, under sufficient background uncertainty.

On the other hand, the second result shows that, for any given level of background uncertainty, one prospect cannot stochastically dominate another when

---

[63] In addition to additive separability between foreground and background components of outcomes, these results rely on the assumptions that background prospects are probabilistically independent of foreground prospects and that they satisfy a "bounded decay" condition roughly equivalent to having exponential or heavier tails. The realism of the latter assumption is defended in §8.1 of Tarsney (2025b).

[64] Related results also appear in Pomatto et al. (2020) and Mu et al. (2024).

its superiority in expected value depends on sufficiently small differences in the probabilities of extreme foreground outcomes.[65] This means that, even in the presence of very high background uncertainty, Stochastic Dominance alone will not require expected value maximization in the context of sufficiently extreme tradeoffs.

It turns out that, given a background prospect with sufficiently heavy tails, Stochastic Dominance will very closely approximate the ranking of prospects by the expected value of their foreground prospects when the dispersion of the background prospect is large relative to the potential stakes of the agent's choice, but will not do so in general when the stakes are large relative to the dispersion of the background prospect.[66] (The "dispersion" of a prospect is how "spread out" its probability mass is, which can be quantified for instance by *interquartile range*, the difference in value between the 25th and 75th percentile outcomes.) The practical significance of these results, then, depends on whether the dispersion of our background prospects is large relative to the foreground stakes in typical real-world choice situations.

Given an impartial additive theory of value, it seems clear that this dispersion should be quite large by any intuitive standard.[67] Consider just one source of background uncertainty, namely the welfare of past welfare subjects on Earth.[68] The size of this population alone is a source of great uncertainty. The past human population, for instance, seems to be roughly $10^{11}$ (Kaneda and Haub, 2022), but with error bars at least on the order of $10^{10}$.[69] Present mammal and vertebrate populations seem to be at least $10^{11}$ and $10^{13}$ respectively (Tomasik, 2019), suggesting historical populations of more than $10^{17}$ and $10^{20}$ respectively (Tarsney and Thomas, 2024, §6.1). And here our uncertainties are even greater – the range of plausible estimates even for *present* mammal and vertebrate populations span multiple orders of magnitude (Tomasik, 2019). In addition, we can say very little about average welfare in any of these populations, including whether it has been positive or negative. Hence, these sources of value alone generate background uncertainties at least on the order of billions

---

[65] In presenting this result, I focus on the simpler case of absolutely small probabilities, but see fn. 22 in Tarsney (2025b) for the application to small probability differences more generally.

[66] For the reasoning behind this claim, and illustrations of what "closely approximate" looks like, see §5.4 of Tarsney (2025b).

[67] The rest of this subsection is largely adapted from Tarsney (2025b).

[68] For arguments from other sources, see Tarsney (2025b, §8.2).

[69] Kaneda and Haub's is the best-known estimate of the number of humans who have ever lived. It involves major simplifying assumptions, like estimating global population at just four points in time before 1200 CE and interpolating population size between those points by assuming a constant growth rate. It has also changed significantly, e.g., from ~108 billion in the 2018 version of their report to 117 billion in the 2022 version.

of human lives. Let's take as our unit of value the value of a typical present-day human life, which we can call a "life equivalent" (LE). In these terms, even if we entirely ignored all nonhuman animals, the dispersion of our background prospects would be at least $10^9$ LE. But it seems reasonable to assume that nonhuman welfare is a source of value, and that the average vertebrate counts for at least one ten-thousandth as much as a human. On these grounds, $10^{14}$ LE seems like a safe lower bound on the dispersion of our real-world background prospects.

If this is right, then any decision theory satisfying Stochastic Dominance must agree with MEV in practice in a very wide range of real-world cases (again, given an impartial additive theory of value). This includes my preferred version of permissivism, but also many versions of anti-fanaticism (e.g., standard forms of Bounded MEU and tail discounting) and versions of fanaticism besides MEV (for instance, unbounded expected utility theories where utility is a nonlinear function of value). If our background uncertainty is at least on the order of $10^{14}$ LE, or even the ultra-conservative $10^9$ LE, then many choices involving intuitively small probability differences and high stakes (e.g., the choice whether to vote in a national election) will plausibly fall into the "small-stakes" domain where Stochastic Dominance requires de facto expected value maximization (i.e., ranking prospects by the expectations of their foreground components, to a close approximation).[70]

What about the question of how to prioritize between existential risk mitigation and safer philanthropic bets? Here the probabilities and stakes can be more extreme, and things are less obvious. Let's consider a choice between a safe bet $S$ that saves a small number of lives $s$ for certain and a long shot $L$ that aims to prevent existential catastrophe, thereby realizing an astronomically large payoff $l$, with only a tiny probability $p$ of success, but with $pl > s$. And assume a background prospect $B$ with the necessary tail properties and an interquartile range at least a couple orders of magnitude larger than $s$.

It turns out that, under plausible assumptions, $L$ will stochastically dominate $S$ given background prospect $B$ if and only if $p$ is greater than approximately $\frac{s}{\text{IQR}(B)}$, the ratio of the sure-thing payoff to the interquartile range

---

[70] Ranking prospects by the expectations of their foreground components is not the same as ranking prospects by their expectations full stop only because, when background prospects are sufficiently heavy-tailed, the overall prospects will not have well-defined expected values. (Background prospects don't need to be this heavy-tailed to give rise to stochastic dominance, though.) Whenever foreground and background prospects all have finite expectations, a prospect's overall expectation is just the sum of the expectations of its foreground and background components, and hence the ranking of options in a given situation by their foreground expectations will agree with the ranking by overall expectations.

of the background prospect (Tarsney, 2025b, 26–27). So for instance, if $s = 10\,\mathrm{LE}$ and $\mathrm{IQR}(B) = 10^{14}\,\mathrm{LE}$, then the probability threshold for stochastic dominance will likely be in the neighborhood of $10^{-13}$.

Are the values of $s$ and $p$ in real-world situations such that $p > \frac{s}{\mathrm{IQR}(B)}$? As noted in Section 8.1, it costs about \$3500 to save a life by funding public health interventions in impoverished countries (GiveWell, 2025). Let's consider, then, an agent who has \$3500 to devote either to global public health or to existential risk mitigation, for whom $s = 1\,\mathrm{LE}$. I argued above that the inter-quartile range of our background uncertainty is at least $10^{14}\,\mathrm{LE}$. This would mean that the probability threshold for stochastic dominance, $\frac{s}{\mathrm{IQR}(B)}$, is $10^{-14}$ or less.

Next, then, how much existential risk mitigation could our agent's \$3500 buy? The relatively conservative estimate of the marginal cost-effectiveness of existential risk mitigation we came up with in Section 8.1 implies an answer of $1.4 \times 10^{-13}$. If we instead used higher estimates of either the baseline level of existential risk or the relative risk reduction that can be purchased for \$1, we could get significantly larger numbers. If we instead worked from Todd's (2017) estimate that \$100 billion could achieve an absolute risk reduction of 1%, still making the conservative assumption of constant returns, we would find that \$3500 could reduce near-term extinction risk by $3.5 \times 10^{-10}$.

As we saw in Section 8.2, though, it's not at all a given that avoiding near-term extinction would result in an astronomically valuable future. So the real value of $p$ is not the probability that $L$ prevents existential catastrophe, but the probability that it prevents existential catastrophe *and* results in the astronomical payoff $l$. My own view is that it would be over-pessimistic to give humanity less than a one-in-a-hundred chance of realizing most of its potential, conditional on surviving the next century. If so, this consideration will lop at most two orders of magnitude off the value of $p$, giving us $p = 1.4 \times 10^{-15}$ on the most conservative estimate, and $3.5 \times 10^{-12}$ if we go by Todd's numbers.

These numbers straddle the probability threshold of $10^{-14}$. But, although there's certainly room for reasonable disagreement, it seems very likely for my money that a careful analysis would find options like $L$ to stochastically dominate options like $S$ in real-world situations like the one we're considering. The $10^{-14}$ threshold was based on the estimate of the dispersion of our background uncertainty at $10^{14}\,\mathrm{LE}$, which strikes me as fairly conservative. And here again higher-order uncertainties are significant: Assigning even one-in-a-hundred probability to an estimate of the cost-effectiveness of existential risk mitigation as optimistic as Todd's would be enough to guarantee that $p > \frac{s}{\mathrm{IQR}(B)}$, given our other assumptions.

If so, then we've reached quite a surprising conclusion! Expected value arguments for prioritizing existential risk mitigation over safer philanthropic bets seemed like a paradigm case of real-world fanaticism. But, plausibly, once we take full account of our real-world circumstances, we can make a case for de facto expected value maximization in this context that rests on no decision-theoretic assumption more controversial than Stochastic Dominance. That case should therefore be embraced by any reasonable decision theory, including anti-fanatical and permissivist theories – even in situations where the effect one can have on the probability of existential catastrophe is, by any intuitive standard, quite small.

Even if this is right, though, the victory of expected value maximization is a limited one. For those who take truly astronomical estimates of the value of the future seriously, expectational arguments for the overwhelming importance of existential risk have implications that extend far beyond philanthropic resource allocation. For instance: At any given moment, it's just barely possible that you are an asymptomatic carrier of a deadly new pathogen capable of causing human extinction, and that humanity's survival depends on whether you pass that pathogen on to anyone else. Should you be willing to make great personal sacrifices to mitigate that risk – for instance, never going to restaurants or concerts, and wearing full personal protective equipment to work every day? If the value of human survival is on the order of $10^{52}$ LE, then MEV might well demand these extreme measures.[71] But here there is still room for permissivists and anti-fanatics to demur. When our choices have only a tenuous connection to existential catastrophe, the ratio between the potential reduction in existential risk and the cost of achieving that reduction is unlikely to exceed the threshold required for stochastic dominance ($\sim 10^{-14}$ per LE, if the interquartile range of our background uncertainty is $10^{14}$ LE). And if it doesn't, then at least as far as Stochastic Dominance is concerned, the magnitude of the stakes is irrelevant. Thus, while we may be forced to agree with expectational arguments for existential risk mitigation in "core" cases like philanthropic resource allocation, the permissivist view sketched in Section 7 can still give us leeway not to follow those arguments to their most fanatical extremes.

---

[71] Suppose there's a one-in-a-billion chance of an extinction-level zoonotic pathogen crossing over to humans in the next century, a one-in-a-million conditional probability that there will be only a single crossover event, a one-in-a-thousand probability of extinction if Patient Zero passes the pathogen to anyone else, and a one-in-ten-billion conditional probability that you'll be Patient Zero. And suppose that a lifetime of precaution would reduce your chance of passing on that pathogen by 50%. Then your precautions could reduce near-term extinction risk by $5 \times 10^{-29}$, for an expected value of $5 \times 10^{23}$ LE!

# 9 Conclusion

Our story has taken several twists and turns, so let's briefly take stock. We've seen prima facie compelling arguments both for and against versions of both fanaticism and anti-fanaticism. I've ultimately concluded that the most persuasive arguments here are negative: against Narrow Fanaticism, and against General Anti-Fanaticism. That led me to endorse Constrained Permissivism, according to which rationality permits both preferences that satisfy Narrow Anti-Fanaticism and incomplete preferences that are neither fanatical nor anti-fanatical. I argued that this picture leaves agents with a great deal of leeway to act like Narrow Fanatics or General Anti-Fanatics, at least in principle, even if it prohibits the fullest realization of either disposition. In the last section, however, I argued that any view that satisfies Stochastic Dominance – including my preferred version of permissivism, and in my opinion any reasonable decision theory – must very often agree with expected value maximization in practice, at least given an impartial additive theory of value. This agreement can run out when probability differences get sufficiently small and stakes get sufficiently extreme. But it may nevertheless vindicate quite a bit of expected value reasoning, including arguments for prioritizing existential risk reduction even when the amount by which one can reduce those risks is quite small by intuitive standards. These conclusions cannot be summarized either as a victory for fanaticism or as a victory for anti-fanaticism. Rationality sometimes requires us to give great weight to small differences in probability (e.g., under high levels of background uncertainty), sometimes places limits on the weight we should give to such differences (e.g., in choices involving St. Petersburg-like prospects), and sometimes leaves it up to us (e.g., in finitary cases involving truly minuscule probability differences). Our job as decision-makers is to figure out which case we're in.

# References


Andreou, C. (2022). *Commitment and Resoluteness in Rational Choice*. Cambridge University Press.

Arntzenius, F., A. Elga, and J. Hawthorne (2004). Bayesianism, infinite decisions, and binding. *Mind 113*(450), 251–283.

Arrow, K. J. (1951). Alternative approaches to the theory of choice in risk-taking situations. *Econometrica 19*(4), 404–437.

Arrow, K. J. (1974). *Essays in the Theory of Risk-Bearing*. North-Holland.

Aumann, R. J. (1977). The St. Petersburg paradox: A discussion of some recent comments. *Journal of Economic Theory 14*(2), 443–445.

Avery, D. T. (2011). Winning the food race. *Brown Journal of World Affairs 18*(1), 107–118.

Bader, R. M. (2018). Stochastic dominance and opaque sweetening. *Australasian Journal of Philosophy 96*(3), 498–507.

Bader, R. M. (2022). Person-affecting utilitarianism. In G. Arrhenius, K. Bykvist, T. Campbell, and E. Finneron-Burns (Eds.), *The Oxford Handbook of Population Ethics*. Oxford University Press, 251–270.

Bales, A., D. Cohen, and T. Handfield (2014). Decision theory for agents with incomplete preferences. *Australasian Journal of Philosophy 92*(3), 453–470.

Balfour, D. (2021). Pascal's mugger strikes again. *Utilitas 33*(1), 118–124.

Barrett, J. (2024). In defense of moderation. *Global Priorities Institute Working Paper Series*. GPI Working Paper No. 32–2024.

Bassett, G. W. (1987). The St. Petersburg paradox and bounded utility. *History of Political Economy 19*(4), 517–523.

Beckstead, N. (2013). *On the Overwhelming Importance of Shaping the Far Future*. Ph. D. thesis, Rutgers University Graduate School, New Brunswick.

Beckstead, N. and T. Thomas (2024). A paradox for tiny probabilities and enormous values. *Noûs 58*(2), 431–455.

Bernoulli, D. (1954 (1738)). Exposition of a new theory on the measurement of risk. *Econometrica 22*(1), 23–36.

Bostrom, N. (2003). Astronomical waste: The opportunity cost of delayed technological development. *Utilitas 15*(3), 308–314.

Bostrom, N. (2009). Pascal's mugging. *Analysis 69*(3), 443–445.

Bostrom, N. (2011). Infinite ethics. *Analysis and Metaphysics 10*, 9–59.

Bostrom, N. (2013). Existential risk prevention as global priority. *Global Policy 4*(1), 15–31.

Bottomley, C. and T. L. Williamson (2024). Rational risk-aversion: Good things come to those who weight. *Philosophy and Phenomenological Research 108*(3), 697–725.

Bottomley, C. and T. L. Williamson (2025). On the offense against fanaticism. *Ethics 135*(2), 320–332.

Buchak, L. (2013). *Risk and Rationality*. Oxford University Press.

Cibinel, P. (2023). A dilemma for Nicolausian discounting. *Analysis 83*(4), 662–672.

Colyvan, M. (2008). Relative expectation theory. *Journal of Philosophy 105*(1), 37–44.

Easwaran, K. (2008). Strong and weak expectations. *Mind 117*(467), 633–641.

GiveWell (2025). Our top charities. Last updated January 2025. www.givewell.org/charities/top-charities.

Goodsell, Z. (2021). A St Petersburg paradox for risky welfare aggregation. *Analysis 81*(3), 420–426.

Goodsell, Z. (2024). Decision theory unbound. *Noûs 58*(3), 669–695.

Greaves, H., T. Thomas, A. Mogensen, and W. MacAskill (2024). On the desire to make a difference. *Philosophical Studies 181*, 1599–1626.

Gustafsson, J. E. (2022). *Money-Pump Arguments*. Cambridge University Press.

Hájek, A. and M. Smithson (2012). Rationality and indeterminate probabilities. *Synthese 187*(1), 33–48.

Hammond, P. J. (1998). Objective expected utility: A consequentialist perspective. *Handbook of Utility Theory 1*, 143–211.

Hare, C. (2010). Take the sugar. *Analysis 70*(2), 237–247.

Henderson, D. A. (2011). The eradication of smallpox – An overview of the past, present, and future. *Vaccine 29*, D7–D9.

Hong, F. (2024). Know your way out of St. Petersburg: An exploration of "knowledge-first" decision theory. *Erkenntnis 89*(6), 2473–2492.

Hong, F. (2025). Fanaticism and knowledge. *Synthese 206*(1), 1–30.

Hong, F., & Russell, J. S. (2025). Paradoxes of infinite aggregation. *Noûs 59*(3), 809–827.

Hurka, T. (1983). Value and population size. *Ethics 93*(3), 496–507.

Irlam, G. (2023). In praise of Viktor Zhdanov. https://80000hours.org/2012/02/in-praise-of-viktor-zhdanov/.

Isaacs, Y. (2016). Probabilities cannot be rationally neglected. *Mind 125*(499), 759–762.

Joyce, J. M. (1999). *The Foundations of Causal Decision Theory*. Cambridge University Press.

Kaneda, T. and C. Haub (2022). How many people have ever lived on earth? Population Reference Bureau. First published in 1997, last updated 2022. www.prb.org/articles/how-many-people-have-ever-lived-on-earth/.

Karger, E., J. Rosenberg, Z. Jacobs et al. (2023). Forecasting existential risks: Evidence from a long-run forecasting tournament. *Forecasting Research Institute Working Paper Series*. FRI Working Paper No. 1. Version dated August 8.

Kosonen, P. (2022). *Tiny Probabilities of Vast Value*. Ph. D. thesis, Worcester College, University of Oxford.

Kosonen, P. (2024). Probability discounting and money pumps. *Philosophy and Phenomenological Research 109*(2), 593–611.

Kowalczyk, K. (forthcoming). Saving fanaticism. *Australasian Journal of Philosophy*.

Machina, M. J. (1982). "Expected utility" analysis without the independence axiom. *Econometrica 50*(2), 277–323.

Mahtani, A. (2017). The ex ante pareto principle. *Journal of Philosophy 114*(6), 303–323.

Mahtani, A. (2024). *The Objects of Credence*. Oxford University Press.

McCarthy, D., K. Mikkola, and T. Thomas (2020). Utilitarianism with and without expected utility. *Journal of Mathematical Economics 87*, 77–113.

Meacham, C. J. G. (2019). Difference minimizing theory. *Ergo 6*(35), 999–1034.

Menger, K. (1979 (1934)). The role of uncertainty in economics. In *Selected Papers in Logic and Foundations, Didactics, Economics*, pp. 259–278. Springer.

Millett, P. and A. Snyder-Beattie (2017). Existential risk and cost-effective biosecurity. *Health Security 15*(4), 373–383.

Monton, B. (2019). How to avoid maximizing expected utility. *Philosophers' Imprint 19*(18), 1–25.

Mu, X., L. Pomatto, P. Strack, and O. Tamuz (2024). Background risk and small-stakes risk aversion. *American Economic Review: Insights 6*(2), 262–276.

Ord, T. (2013). The moral imperative toward cost-effectiveness in global health. Center for Global Development Essay. www.cgdev.org/content/publications/detail/1427016.

Ord, T. (2020). *The Precipice: Existential Risk and the Future of Humanity*. Bloomsbury.

Pascal, B. (1852 (1669)). *Pensées*. Dezobry et E. Magdeleine.

Peterson, M. (2023). The St. Petersburg Paradox. In E. N. Zalta and U. Nodelman (Eds.), *The Stanford Encyclopedia of Philosophy* (Fall ed.). Metaphysics Research Lab, Stanford University.

Pomatto, L., P. Strack, and O. Tamuz (2020). Stochastic dominance under independent noise. *Journal of Political Economy 128*(5), 1877–1900.

Rees, M. (2003). *Our Final Century: Will the Human Race Survive the Twenty-first Century?* William Heinemann.

Ross, J. (2006). Rejecting ethical deflationism. *Ethics 116*(4), 742–768.

Russell, J. S. (2023). On two arguments for fanaticism. *Noûs 58*(3), 565–595.

Russell, J. S. (forthcoming). Fixing stochastic dominance. *The British Journal for the Philosophy of Science.*

Russell, J. S. and Y. Isaacs (2021). Infinite prospects. *Philosophy and Phenomenological Research 103*(1), 178–198.

Sagan, C. (1994). *Pale Blue Dot: A Vision of the Human Future in Space* (1st ed.). Random House.

Savage, L. J. (1972). *The Foundations of Statistics* (2nd ed.). Dover.

Schoenfield, M. (2014). Decision making in the face of parity. *Philosophical Perspectives 28*(1), 263–277.

Seidenfeld, T., M. J. Schervish, and J. B. Kadane (2009). Preference for equivalent random variables: A price for unbounded utilities. *Journal of Mathematical Economics 45*, 329–340.

Smart, J. J. C. (1956). Extreme and restricted utilitarianism. *Philosophical Quarterly 6*(25), 344–354.

Smith, N. J. J. (2014). Is evaluative compositionality a requirement of rationality? *Mind 123*(490), 457–502.

Spears, D. and M. Geruso (2025). *After the Spike: Population, Progress, and the Case for People.* Simon & Schuster.

Tarsney, C. (2023). The epistemic challenge to longtermism. *Synthese 201*(6), 1–37.

Tarsney, C. (2025a). Against anti-fanaticism. *Philosophy and Phenomenological Research 110*(2), 734–753.

Tarsney, C. (2025b). Expected value, to a point: Moral decision-making under background uncertainty. *Noûs 59*(4), 1093–1125.

Tarsney, C., Lederman, H., & Spears, D. (2025). A Dominance Argument Against Incompleteness. *Philosophical Review 134*(4), 455–490.

Tarsney, C. and T. Thomas (2024). Non-additive axiologies in large worlds. *Ergo 11*(9), 238–287.

Temkin, L. S. (2022). *Being Good in a World of Need.* Oxford University Press.

Thorstad, D. (2023). High risk, low reward: A challenge to the astronomical value of existential risk mitigation. *Philosophy and Public Affairs 51*(4), 373–412.

Thorstad, D. (2024). Mistakes in the moral mathematics of existential risk. *Ethics 135*(1), 122–150.

Todd, B. (2017). The case for reducing existential risks. 80,000 Hours. https://80000hours.org/articles/extinction-risk/.

Todd, B. (2023). How much do solutions to social problems differ in their effectiveness? A collection of all the studies we could find. https://80000hours.org/2023/02/how-much-do-solutions-differ-in-effectiveness/.

Tomasik, B. (2019). How many wild animals are there? First published 2009, updated August 7, 2019. https://reducing-suffering.org/how-many-wild-animals-are-there/.

Trammell, P. and L. Aschenbrenner (2024). Existential risk and growth. *Global Priorities Institute Working Paper Series*. GPI Working Paper No. 13-2024.

von Neumann, J. and O. Morgenstern (1947). *Theory of Games and Economic Behavior* (2nd ed.). Princeton University Press.

Wagner, G. and M. L. Weitzman (2015). *Climate Shock: The Economic Consequences of a Hotter Planet*. Princeton University Press.

Wilkinson, H. (2022). In defense of fanaticism. *Ethics 132*(2), 445–477.

Wilkinson, H. (2023). Infinite aggregation and risk. *Australasian Journal of Philosophy 101*(2), 340–359.

Wilkinson, H. (2024). Egyptology and fanaticism. *Philosophical Studies 181*(8), 1903–1923.

Wilkinson, H. (2025). Flummoxing expectations. *Noûs 59*(3), 700–728.

For EU product safety concerns, contact us at Calle de José Abascal, 56–1°,
28003 Madrid, Spain or eugpsr@cambridge.org.

www.ingramcontent.com/pod-product-compliance
Lightning Source LLC
LaVergne TN
LVHW010912030626
840340LV00033B/660